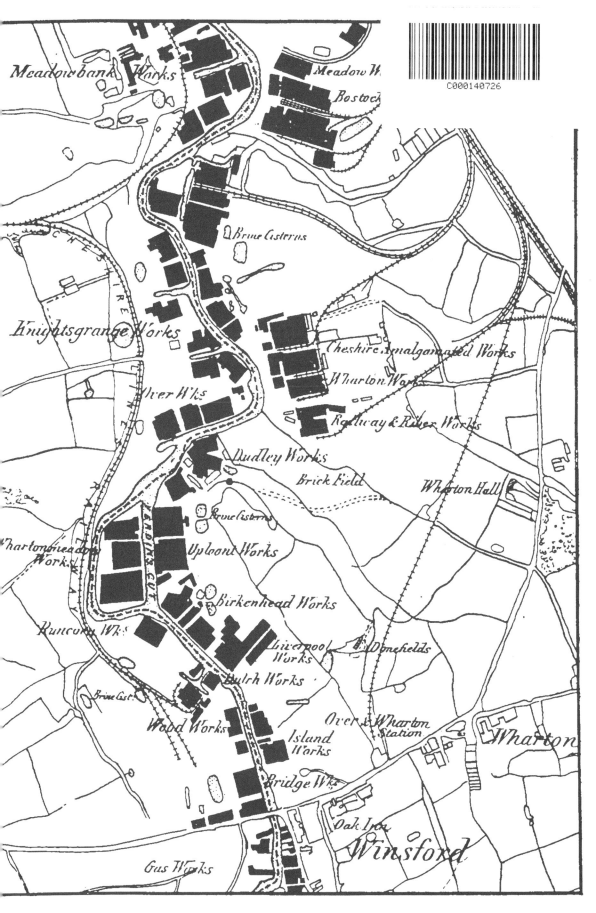

Meadowbank Works

Meadow W.

Bostock

C000140726

CHESHIRE

Brine Cisterns

Knightsgrange Works

Cheshire Amalgamated Works

Over Wks

Wharton Work

Railway & River Works

Dudley Works

Brick Field

Wharton Hall

VARDEN'S CUT

Brine Cisterns

Whartonmeadow Works

Uploont Works

Birkenhead Works

Runcorn Wks

Liverpool Works

Dorfields

Dutch Works

Over & Wharton Station

Wharton

Wood Works

Island Works

Brine Cist.

Bridge Wks

Oak Iron

Winsford

Gas Works

The Book of Winsford 1997
has been published
as a Limited Edition
of which this is

Number **23**/

A list of original
subscribers is printed
at the back
of this book

FRONT COVER: The Salt Union Works at Meadow Bank around 1900. Each shed contained a single salt pan and each pan had its own chimney, burning poor quality low-cost coal. There must have been more industrial chimneys in this small area than anywhere else on earth of comparable size.

Recreation

Beauty

Legend

Industry

Transportation

Views of Winsford in 1958, from the Council Chairman's Christmas
Card.

THE BOOK OF
WINSFORD

BY

J. BRIAN CURZON

BA MA (Arch) (Mus Stud) MEd AMA

BARON
MCMXMCVII

PUBLISHED BY BARON BIRCH FOR QUOTES LIMITED
AND PRODUCED BY KEY COMPOSITION,
SOUTH MIDLANDS LITHOPLATES, CHENEY & SONS,
HILLMAN PRINTERS (FROME) & WBC BOOK MANUFACTURERS

ISBN 0 86023 580 7

Contents

Acknowledgements

I have collected information on old Winsford since I was a schoolboy but the task of writing this history meant organising many facts into a meaningful story and weaving disparate strands into a worthwhile study.

It is often difficult to reach the truth about the local past, which derives from many sources which were never intended to be historical. They were simply the documents or buildings required for the work of the day. One has only to read the two town newspapers to get the impression that they come from different areas. However, this is a personal view and no doubt others will form their own.

I would like to thank the various people who have checked the drafts of this text. Each has suggested improvements and spotted typing errors, besides adding extra information. Tony Bostock MA, Joan Beck MA and Colin Walsh of the Local History Society, Dr Robin Studd of the Keele University Local History Centre, Bob Curzon of the *Guardian*, Stephen Penney BA, Curator of the Salt Museum, Vera Barton and Nicholas Wilson from old local families, along with the entire Town Council, have all had an opportunity to comment on the text before publication.

Nick Hughes BSc of the DAN organisation has helped make production easier by allowing use of their sophisticated computer equipment, and in many other ways. The Editor of the *Chronicle*, Dave Fox BA, and photographer Tony Clixby, have helped with illustrations and have taken many photos especially for the book, making them a special record of the present. Some photos have come from work conducted in the town by the former Northwich Archaeology Group.

Much support has come from local people who have provided oral history, often over a drink in a pub, and passed on their memories over many years. It is difficult to ensure that such material is factual and not a matter of opinion. As with the folklore of the town one can only offer a conclusion, but without such information there would be no complete book.

The anonymous loan of the Vale Royal and Darnhall estate books from the 1850s has been invaluable. An anonymous donation of glass negatives taken in Winsford around 1900 has been a source of several illustrations but the negatives have been passed on to the Salt Museum for protection. The staff at Winsford and Northwich Libraries have also provided invaluable help as well as illustrations.

However, the book remains a personal analysis of the information available and makes no claims to be an exclusively correct and indisputable history.

Key to Caption Credits

C	*Chronicle*		MM	Manchester Museum
CL	Cheshire Libraries		NAG	Former Northwich Archaeology Group
CM	Cheshire Museums		SO	Susan Orme
GC	Gerard Conealey		SU	Salt Union
GMC	Grosvenor Museum, Chester		TS	Trevor Sayle
H	Mr & Mrs Hodkinson		THAG	Towneley Hall Art Gallery, Burnley
ICI	ICI Ltd		WTC	Winsford Town Council
MB	Mary Berry			

Foreword

by Nicholas Wilson

For anyone with a love for, or an interest in, central Cheshire, Brian Curzon's *Book of Winsford* makes fascinating reading. The research undertaken has been thorough and dedicated, as anyone who reads his articles in *The Chronicle* could tell you. It should prove to be an illuminating and informative introduction for future research students wishing to pursue any aspect of Winsford's history in greater depth.

Reading it has brought back many happy memories, and given me a greater understanding of the problems, trials and tribulations that faced the town's population over so many years. It was my grandfather's (and father's) interest in engineering and minerals that brought our family to the town over eighty years ago. During this rather short time – in historical terms – so many changes have taken place as highlighted by Brian. I doubt if RWW (my grandfather) would be able to recognise it as the base of his first industrial undertaking. I suspect that, as Winsford continues to evolve over the next eighty years, future generations of my family may ponder the question as to why we took such an active interest in its development. The answer is simple: the town has been a large part of our lives, there have been happy and sad times but, whatever the situation, it has always been the centre to which we have returned; to the friendships that have developed in all walks of life and to the tranquillity of its immediately surrounding environment. As the Borough Council's logo states, it is the very heart of Cheshire – and it is steeped in a long and unique history.

So many people have played their part in the changes and growth of the town, some would say not always for the better, that it is impossible to mention them all. The strength of Winsford has always been the infinite capacity of the resident population to adapt and build community life whatever the difficulties that have confronted them. This I believe is the underlying message in this book. I pay tribute to the people of the town, many of whose families have been here for generations, for the part they have played in its progress and to Brian for chronicling it so well.

Wharton Hall
Winsford

Dedication

In memory of my parents, both Old Winfordians

Winsford

Progressions twain, of beauty and of use.
Prospect within, without.
Who has a seeker's eye
Will journey hereabout.
Down in the Vale.
Amid the town
Trade pulses its increase;
See here works where the Weaver winding goes,
And traffic most of brine
With pungency of strength,
Moves to a world's long line.
Shaped is the face of empty space
By wise extensions power,
And near, as with a dreamy timepiece tick,
Passes a soft enchanting hour.

Headley Lucas
1939

The badge of Winsford was designed by John Henry Cooke and uses the Over mace as a crest with the arms of Vale Royal Abbey, Cheshire (inverted!) and Verdin; the fourth quarter represents three salt barrows dripping brine. The Motto translates as 'Virtue is the safest defence': the Verdin motto. It is not recognised by the College of Heralds.

Introducing Winsford

Winsford is my birthplace and home, there have been Curzons here for centuries, and I have intended to write its history since I was at school in the 1960s. This volume makes no claim to be the definitive history or even a work of original scholarship. It is an introduction to an interesting town from earliest times to the redevelopment of the last 30 years. Winsford is situated just west of Bostock where an oak tree marks the traditional centre of Cheshire.

There is clearly enough scope for constant research into the town's history and any one chapter could be developed into a veritable thesis. However, this book is aimed to interest and entertain those who desire to know more about the place where they live. Only introductory chapters on such subjects as the history of Vale Royal, the Weaver Navigation and the salt industry are included, but they should also be of use to students and pupils, who could develop a given chapter into a project for examination by using the bibliography.

It is important to stress that there was no such place as Winsford until the 18th century. To all intents and purposes Over and Wharton were completely separate villages (Winsford was included with Wharton up to the late 19th century). From the mid-1960s Winsford has developed, first as an overspill town for Manchester, then Liverpool, and more recently as a setting for privately owned houses as modern roads have made it something of a commuter town. It is easy to forget that it has an historic core and that over a dozen mediaeval settlements existed in the area covered by this book.

Whitegate and Moulton are both included where relevant as they are part of the developing history of the town and were once part of the Local Board or UDC.

Both Over and Wharton are mentioned in Domesday Book (1086) along with Weaver, Conersley (Whitegate), Little Budworth, Darnhall, Wettenhall and Moulton. Those on the west of the river belonged to the Earl of Chester and those on the east to the Baron of Shipbrook. Winsford was simply the crossing point between the two until 1721, when the River Weaver was made navigable, though Winsford Bridge is mentioned in a 14th century document. Men on the boats which came to the ever-growing salt works would talk for the first time of going to Winsford. It was an area in its own right by the middle of the century. Even so, it is still claimed that the only house in Winsford is the Red Lion at Winsford Bridge, as all others are either in Over or Wharton.

In historic terms Over was a parish and borough in its own right, while Wharton was a hamlet in a remote part of Davenham parish. The boundaries of the ancient hundreds and later Parliamentary divisions separated them along the river.

In the 13th century the mighty Abbey of Vale Royal was founded north of Winsford and this was to change the way of life of local people. Winsford has seen three redevelopments as a new town, first in the 13th century as a new borough, then in the 19th century as a boom town, and from the '60s as a designated development area. Twice, in the 14th and 19th centuries, local men and women have made a dramatic defence against oppression.

In the last couple of decades new roads have provided a direct route through the town, mainly tree-lined dual carriageways. Winsford is only five miles from the M6 and is linked to it by modern roads. There can be no better illustration of the changes than the street maps inside the cover.

The River Weaver was used to carry coal to the salt works and take salt to Liverpool but this trade ended around 40 years ago. The Weaver, today, is used by pleasure craft, anglers and walkers on the tow-path. South of Winsford Bridge the Flashes were created during the last century by collapses into underground brine springs. Today they are a centre for yachting and caravanning.

The prevailing winds are warm wet south-westerlies. They lose much of their water passing over the Welsh mountains, while north winds blow through the Cheshire gap to deposit snow in Shropshire. Mid-Cheshire escapes extremes of climate.

Since 1974 Winsford has been part of the Vale Royal District, later Borough, which has its modern office buildings in the town. These were opened in1991 by Princess Margaret. The name Wyvern House refers to the heraldic beast on the Borough crest. It is an heraldic pun on the river name.

The Town Council occupies a suite at Wyvern House. The Mayor wears the red robe and chain and is preceded by the maces of Winsford and Over. It remains 'the town in the country'; surrounded by some of Cheshire's prettiest villages and attractive countryside in 'England's Greenest County'.

This book is devoted to telling the tale of Winsford and to making people aware of its heritage.

Filling the pointed 'salt barrows' as are shown on the Winsford badge.

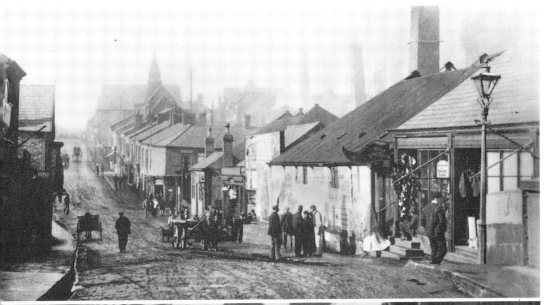

ABOVE: 'The bottom of Winsford', c1900, a salt works on the right with the chimneys of Hamlett's works beyond, behind the Navigation Church. The filthy state of the road was caused by horse traffic. (CM) BELOW: 'The bottom of Winsford', c1960 shows the Co-op shops on the right and the non-stop traffic using the single bridge. The present one was built in 1929 and cost £5,000 but a bridge has existed here since at least the 14th century.

ABOVE: Wharton Hill, 1892: most of the property is long gone. Sometimes this is called Winsford Hill, but sometimes Gravel or High Street are given the same name in old documents. (CL) BELOW: Station Road 1892: working class housing built on a pleasant site overlooking the Flashes and well away from the smoking steamy salt works. A German visitor once compared such housing to French loaves cut into slices. (CL)

Rock of Ages

The origin of Winsford's past prosperity lies in two beds of almost pure salt underneath the town. They were formed in conditions resembling the Dead Sea. Shallow, possibly seasonal, water in an inland sea was replenished by streams and/or tides for unknown centuries. This was in the Triassic period around 200 million years ago. Because of continental drift the area was then situated near the equator and not dissimilar from today's Sahara. The sun continually dried the water, leaving thick deposits of salt. Sand storms blew layers of dust and ash into the water and at other times it was clear. This caused bands of different colours in the rock salt which resembles old-fashioned sweets when crushed. The process occurred twice, creating two layers of salt.

Those beds are separated by a bed of Keuper Marl, which is hardened desert sands, indicating that the water supply had completely dried up. The miners called this 'metal'. The rock salt is found around 80 and 120 metres below the surface; the lower bed produces the finest salt from 700 feet below the countryside. To avoid risk of flooding from old workings, the mine chambers expand from under the Industrial Estate to a fault following King Street in Middlewich and as far north as Whatcroft near Davenham. This avoids any risk of subsidence damage or noise from explosives as there is little property above.

No fossils have ever been found, as the ancient sea was too salty for life to survive. The modern mine is airy at a constant 45 degrees F. It contains no explosive gases and each working section is 65 feet wide and 25 feet high, separated by 80 feet square columns.

Early mining of the top bed in Winsford was not successful as brine streams soon flooded the workings. Two mines were operating in the 1850s but Winsford's only remaining one closed in 1892 because Northwich mines were easier and less costly to operate and could more than cope with falling demand. It was the development of the motor car and demand for rock salt for snow clearance which saw the Meadow Bank Mine reopen in 1929. Today's mine has 130 miles of glistening underground highways and is worked by giant excavators and trucks. The days of pick axes and pit ponies are long gone.

It is the upper bed, which was dissolved by natural water to form brine, that once provided the source of Winsford's wealth. Salt was made from 'wild brine' – natural streams flowing over the rock salt. Where the water enters the rock it dissolves it, but further along the journey it can hold no more and the rock salt is unaffected. At the places where water seeped in, underground caves formed and then collapsed. This caused surface hollows which soon filled with water and are known as Flashes, from the old English word for flooded grassland.

The first recorded subsidence was in 1731 when picnickers from Weaver Hall were disturbed by rumblings and thundering underground. They barely escaped when a vast chasm opened up as they fled. They were convinced that the very gates of Hell were opening behind them. Then the waters of the Weaver broke through their banks to fill the hole. This became the Top Flash (now almost silted up). Throughout the 19th century the run of brine, almost directly under the river, dissolved the salt and the pools got longer and wider. Once known as the 'Cheshire Broads', they form one of the most attractive landscape features of the town, even though the 'bungalows' at the Cheshire Broads site were little better than sheds and some of the worst slums in Cheshire between the Wars.

The Ice Ages scraped any later geological cover away. A river running from a cave in the melting ice is believed to have formed the long deposit of fine bedded sand which runs from Delamere to Nantwich along the Over Ridge. This is noted for dairy farming and early potato crops, including the favourite 'Whitegates' and has been exploited for building sand.

Most important for human occupation, the sand is mainly sealed under boulder clay and acts as a huge sponge. This 'aquifer' has influenced human settlement for generations. The moats at Knights and Marton Granges were fed from it. Wells were at St Chad's, Well Street and another fed the factory boilers of the old cotton mills there. There are many natural streams rising along this spring line, and some feed actual brooks. There are others such as Dene Brook, running in a culvert between the shopping centre and council offices. Springs which wet the pavement in front of the Abbott's Way shops and on Laurel Bank and Hazel Drive on the Dene Estate are less obviously natural. The water once provided the main ingredient for the Over Brewery and a mineral water factory in Delamere Street.

The sand was covered by layers of boulder clay as the ice-sheets melted. The underlying sand is deeper the further down the hill you go. Rounded stones in the clay were transported from Scotland and the Lake District and were polished by ice action on the way. The small ones became cobbles for road making; larger ones were often placed beside buildings to protect them from cart wheels. Two of these large 'erratics', which were formerly at the entrance to Clough Row, have been retained by the entrance to the old High Street from the dual carriageway.

Boulder clay was used from the earliest occupation until the 18th century for wattle and daub – one Over mayor was reputedly a dauber. Some examples of 17th century cottages with wattle and daub walls survive along the Over Ridge. From the early 17th century clay was used for brick-making. Large brick works were between the High Street and Dingle Lane in Victorian times, and the Vale Royal estate books show that kilns were set up near larger new buildings to save the cost of transport. Excavations on the site of Marton Grange found ample evidence of wasters and kiln debris; bricks were made there for the farm in 1840 as estate book accounts confirm. The name Kilnhouses, opposite the Gate Inn, records brickworks or a pottery. This use of local materials gave the older parts of town some architectural unity.

Almost every field in the district had a marl pit, where farmers dug this clay to scatter on sandy soil and waterlogged ground. They held water for animals to drink. They are clearly marked on large scale maps as are the long plantations winding along stream sides or following roads. Examination of field patterns shows groupings of small regular shaped fields around the old village centres, where strips have been enclosed, and larger fields beyond, showing later forest clearance. The Vale Royal Abbey's own fields are larger since the monks were not subject to strip farming.

The action of the ice-sheets piled moraine on the Shropshire border. This forced the Weaver to turn from its southerly course to flow directly north. It is one of the few rivers in the world to do so.

It has been suggested that the Weaver was used by Neolithic traders around 5000 BC, who carried axes from North Wales and the Lake District into central England, using the river to reach the headwaters of the Severn or *via* the Dane to the Trent. There is also a suggestion of an ancient route following the Over Ridge. A flint arrowhead and blade have been found in Swanlow Lane and the names Swanlow and Earnslow testify to vanished burial mounds. Others exist, as at Moulton (overlooking the river) and Hartford, indicating Bronze Age occupation.

However, there is little evidence to support the suggestion of a Roman road leaving the Chester to York road in Delamere. It is said to cross the Weaver at Winsford and to pass through Middlewich on the way to Buxton. No archaeological trace has ever been found apart from a suggested junction in Delamere. If it existed, it headed for Salterswall and then turned along the Over Ridge before going down Welsh Lane to the Weaver crossing. Roman roads do not normally make turnings like that and the route is not even shown on Burdett's 1777 map.

A more likely origin of the route lies in the names of Welsh Lane and Salterswell. This was a pack horse road used in mediaeval and post-mediaeval times to take salt to Chester and North Wales. Stepping stones at the ford existed in the 18th century. The remarkably straight road from Delamere to the outskirts of Winsford is only one of several straight roads in the forest. They were created when it was enclosed in the 18th century. The presence of a toll house near Salterswall is a reminder that this was a turn-pike road and it was almost certainly the trustees and foresters who were responsible for the straight road, and not the Romans.

The name Salterswall (Salterswell) perhaps explains the reason for the diversion, for a natural spring there would have provided the last watering hole for pack animals crossing the forest. It is first recorded in 1344.

However, a hoard of Roman coins is recorded as being found near Winsford in the 18th century and a number of Roman objects were said to have been found when New Bridge was altered in the 1830s. The author has also seen a couple of Roman coins which, it was claimed, were found at Salterswall and which the finder retained. This suggests agricultural activity on Romano-British farms in the area.

The road was almost certainly part of a route used in the Middle Ages, known as the Earl's route, by which the Earl of Chester could travel to London *via* Congleton and Leek and stop over at one of his own properties each night.

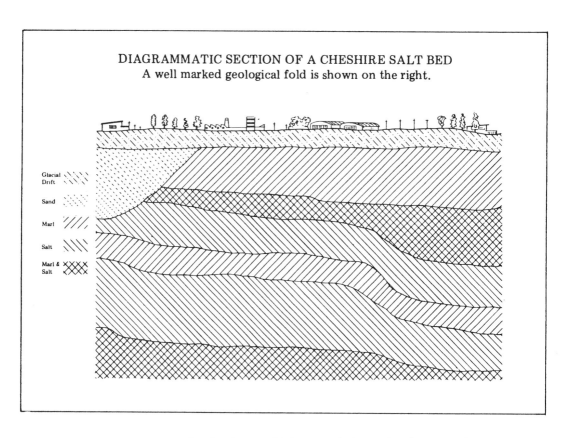

DIAGRAMMATIC SECTION OF A CHESHIRE SALT BED
A well marked geological fold is shown on the right.

Glacial Drift
Sand
Marl
Salt
Marl & Salt

The suggested Triassic sea which created the rock salt – a section
through the salt beds. (ICI)

16

ABOVE: Already obsolete, this 25 ft high monster was used to remove loose rock salt from the roof of the tunnels. Its metal is so corroded by the salt that recovery was not worth while and it was left in the mine. BELOW: Excavating machine in the mine – the size can be calculated from the driver's cab. (SU)

ABOVE: Local materials for local buildings, timber and brick nogging at the side, local brick at the front, this cottage would have had a Cheshire straw thatch, not Norfolk reed. The chimneys are a Victorian fantasy addition and a glacial erratic boulder protects the corner. (NAG) BELOW: Falcon Cottage at Marton is typical of the 17th century cottages of the 'rebuilding' era which were once numerous along the road from Whitegate to Church Minshull. (NAG)

King's Vale and Tall Tales

The first mention of the locality in writing are references to the estates of Over and Wharton in the Domesday Book of 1086, along with surrounding villages. Each settlement had a handful of peasant holdings, a few acres of ploughland and a wood which was taxable. Both Over and Wharton are on high land on the east and west of the river. The valley floor would have been liable to regular flooding until the creation of the Weaver Navigation, and no occupation was recorded there. A Winsford Bridge was mentioned as early as 1344. Many names in daily use today, such as Bradford (*broad-ford*) (1240), Woodford (1240) and Littler (Little Over) (1260) are mentioned in mediaeval documents.

Many place-names date from before Domesday Book. Like most Cheshire rivers the Weaver has a Celtic name, indicating its former winding course. Over too, is Celtic – one of the oldest place-names in the county, indicating a settlement on a hill. Darnhall is Saxon from *dern* (hidden) and *hale* (hole), or hidden hollow. Swanlow probably refers to a lost burial mound and is derived from *swain* (pigs) *lowe*.

Marton was a *ton* (settlement) at a *mere* (boundary) and is Saxon, while Whitegate is a mediaeval name indicating its place at the gate of the white monks. Wharton had its distant origins as *Weaver-ton*, but was corrupted through *Waverton* to the present version. An alternative view that it derives from a waving tree is not convincing; Winsford is a Saxon word. The interpretation of it as *Wainsford* (wagon ford) can be discounted as pack horses were preferred at that time. The more usually accepted interpretation is that Win was the name of someone living by the ford.

The fact that no mention is made of St Chad's church in Domesday could simply imply that it did not pay tax. Christian worship took place on the valley site at least 200 years before Domesday, as the fragment of an Anglo Saxon cross, which is preserved beside the organ, testifies.

Several churches in Cheshire are dedicated to St Chad, which may mark places where he preached on his pilgrimages around the then new Lichfield diocese. There are several wells in and around the church: St Chad is associated with sacred wells throughout his diocese. Wells near churches often indicate a pagan origin as they were used for water worship in fertility cults. This is reinforced by the churchyard, for aerial photos and early maps show it to lie within an originally circular churchyard – the northern part now converted to a car-park. This too is often associated with pagan origins, perhaps as a sacred grove in the forest. The naming of the adjoining parishes in honour of Chad's contemporaries, Wilfred and Boniface, indicates that these parishes were created by succeeding generations when memories were fresh.

St Chad's secluded site in a valley suggests further evidence of a foundation in unsettled times, for pagans (*eg* Vikings) passing along the road would see no sign of it hidden in the trees. In the 1960s it held the record for the longest bell-ringing session, perhaps the lack of neighbours the reason for the attempt!

Our earliest written knowledge of the church dates from the time when Randle de Keveliok, Earl of Chester, presented it to St Mary's Convent in Chester. The grant was renewed by his successor Randle De Blundevelle. Keveliok also granted the estate which became known as the Nun House, in Wharton, to the convent. His daughter, Amica, is believed to have been married in the church. It was the legitimacy of this lady and her marriage which caused continual litigation in the 17th century as this affected the legitimacy of most of Cheshire's noble pedigrees.

Over Church was one of few churches where sanctuary was legally recognised, which suggests that the church was the senior, if not the oldest, in the forest of Mara. The Earl's interest was prompted by his attendance at his summer hunting lodge at Darnhall, in the forest half a mile to the east. He was also Lord of the Manor of Over. The siting of the church was for his convenience; inconvenience for the villagers was not a consideration.

Mention of forests at Darnhall and Marton in 13th century documents indicate that the extensive forests of Mondrum and Mara then extended right into the later Winsford district. Over was and still is the first real settlement after Kelsall on the A54. It indicates the forest restrictions continued in force for many years. There is a ward in local council elections which has the name Mara to this day.

The last Norman Earl, John le Scot, died in Darnhall in 1237, probably poisoned by his Welsh wife, Princess Helen. She had hoped to become Countess of Chester, but the earldom was held by Henry III until his son, Edward, was created Earl of Chester in 1255. He became lord of the manors of Over, Darnhall, Marton, Conersley and a host of other Cheshire manors. He intended to use his manor house and hunting lodge at Darnhall for the foundation of this Abbey, to which monks moved in 1273. The manor house provided them with temporary accommodation, but how much, if any, building took place is unknown. It has been claimed 'that amongst the woods and waters it was not, forsooth, pleasant and lightsome enough for their fat worships'.

Eight grange farms – Knights (or Beurepair), Darnhall, Hefferstone, Earnslow, Conersley, Marton, Bradford and Sutton – were founded. They provided food for the Abbey and work for the lay brothers. Their numbers were decreasing from the 13th century. Knights' Grange was apparently occupied by them, as 'knight' in this case refers to such workers or to young men (novices?), not to a titled man. They normally lived in or near the Abbey but did not take full vows and were labourers rather than scholars. Occupation here may have been when the church was being built and the residential part of the Abbey was in temporary quarters. By the end of the Middle Ages it was let as a working farm.

Marton Grange was obtained by an exchange of land by the de Mertons in 1328. Earlier John de Merton was fined £10 at the Chester court of 1271-2. This and other local fines for woodland clearance was more of a licence to clear woodland for agriculture than a fine for wrong-doing. Reference to woodlands in this and an earlier record of c1220 with the name, Marton infra Mara, indicates that this was a period of forest clearance, known as assarting. Later the Abbey had the rights of assarting in the forest. The documents concerning the exchange are given in Ormerod's *Cheshire*: a licence from Prince Edward to give permission for the exchange, Merton's quitclaim to Edward I, a grant by the King to Vale Royal, another by the King, of Gayton in Wirral and Lache on Rudheath to Merton. The documents are particularly detailed and were drawn up at the Royal court, not locally.

Little mediaeval occupation was traced in an extensive dig at Marton and the conclusion was that the site had been used as and when needed but not permanently occupied. At Marton, the remains of a drawbridge can still be detected. A moat is fed from one of the natural springs on the spring-line. Water flows from it into two hollows interpreted as the 'fishery' mentioned in the 1328 transactions. From the ponds it flowed through the former village site at Gale Green, providing water supply and waste disposal. Next it fed the pool serving the Abbot's mill at Bradford. Sand banks deposited by it would have been the base for the broad ford itself. It was an intensive use of a short length of water. A smaller excavation at Knights Grange traced a moat, but no structures, though medieval pottery was found.

The Abbot maintained another mill at Darnhall, where a later mill and associated buildings survive as an attractive grouping in the wooded valley. A weir held back an extensive mill pool behind, which split into a tributary in the woods, forming a pool at an angle to the main pool. Water was held back here as a reservoir and the pool was used for boating and fishing in the Victorian period. In the present century it was a traditional destination for country walks, ending in a splash-about. The weir was breached in the '70s because of fears of drowning. This partially fulfilled the prophecy of (local prophet) Robert Nixon who claimed the pond would become a lane. A cattle track goes along the former pool bed today.

Being forced to use the Abbey mills (and pay tolls) was one of the grievances men from Darnhall tried to put before the King, but the monks needed every penny to pay building and running costs. Over the next three and a half centuries the estates were intensively farmed for grain and livestock. Much of the forest was cleared, apart from woods left for timber and fuel.

The romantic picture painted by people like John Henry Cooke in his book *Ida*, of the King choosing a beautiful valley and calling it Vale Royal is contrary to the Cistercian ethos. They were only allowed to settle on poor land that no one else wanted and to bring this into cultivation as a sign of humility. They had to have a church without ornament far away from the distractions of towns. Although the settlement of Conersley was probably near the site before the monks obtained it, there was poor sandy land at the edge of the forest. Much forest clearance must have been undertaken just to supply building materials for the workmen's huts, temporary buildings for the monks and the church itself.

Edward never called the district 'Vale Royal' because of its beautiful valley. Ideas of natural beauty were unknown in mediaeval times because everywhere was natural – such notions are a post-Renaissance invention. During his reign it was always referred to as *Vallis Regallis* and the Anglicised Vale Royal only emerged after the Reformation. He did say that he wanted 'no other Abbey in the world to be more Royal in liberties, wealth and honour', but that is far removed from scenic delights.

The monks were concerned with maintaining an efficient estate, not how it looked. The present grassy, well-wooded prospect is mainly 'romantic' planting by the first Baron Delamere. Riverside sites were preferred by Cistercian monks, who used them for waste disposal as well as fishing. Monks used large stone-lined drains to carry waste to the river. Later discovery of one of these started stories of secret passages. Such tales are associated with old structures throughout the country but few have any substance.

Besides their agricultural interests the monks engaged in craft and industry. The records of building paid for by the King are particularly detailed. He spent around £30,000. Custom was given to local people such as the smith at Tarvin, who made hatchets. Stone was quarried from Eddisbury Hill and records of each cartload remain. The roads must have been improved to take so much traffic. The probable route was along the disused drive from the Round Tower, through the New Park. A 'green road' still follows the track and other mediaeval routes can be traced as grassy paths in the fields.

The monks had a stained glass workshop, which has been located by archaeologists in Kingswood at Delamere, and a bloomery (iron smelting hearth) which may have been the origin for the furnace working in the 17th century.

No account of Winsford would be complete without mention of Robert Nixon (or Old Nick's son), the palatine prophet. There are various versions of this traditional tale and little to confirm it. One says he lived at the time of Henry VII, the other claims James I. Born at Bark House on Grange Lane or Bridge End House, he was said to be an illiterate ploughboy hardly able to utter single-syllable words. He is said to have 'seen' the battle of Bosworth and shouted instructions to Henry and Richard.

He was taken to the Abbey where he prophesied its end: a small thorn sapling was to become the Abbey door and he was ridiculed for that. At the Dissolution the old thorn bush was cut down and used to prevent animals straying into the ruins. He said that Norton Priory and Vale Royal would meet in the middle of the Weaver – this came true when Acton Bridge was built with stone from the two buildings. Perhaps the prophesy with the most convincing ring of truth was that which said that enemies would attack Britain with fire from Germany, Denmark and Norway. Printed in the 17th century, this could be a prophecy of the Blitz.

Word of Nixon reached the King. He was summoned to the Royal Court. He refused to go, saying he would starve to death. The King ordered he be kept in the Royal kitchen, where he made a nuisance of himself stealing food, so the cook locked him in a cupboard to keep him out of mischief. The cook was called away on business, and so Nixon died as he had prophesied, surrounded by plenty.

The original text recording the prophet was ordered by the Abbot, and is said to have been kept at Vale Royal. It was first reproduced at the time of the Glorious Revolution in the 17th century; as such its nostrums were interpreted as good omens for the Anglicans after James II was deposed. The favourite was that a raven would nest in the stone lion's mouth before a British King was expelled from the country, never to return. Many remembered a raven nesting in a gargoyle on St Chad's Church just before the flight of James II. Now the palatine prophet is enshrined in local legend.

Another tall tale tells how Friar Francis outwitted the Devil, who offered anything he wanted for his soul. The friar demanded food and drink for the rest of his life and a dozen hay bands (ropes for binding the harvest), which had to be grown on Marton Sands. Satan was unable to produce one. An annual festival of ploughing the sands was held until last century to prevent him ever doing so.

The local tale of which most people have heard of is that of Ida. Few who tell it have actually taken the trouble to read it and many ridiculous versions are told which have been invented down the years or mixed with other tales. It relates to a monument set up in 1813 using a stone from one of the Abbey columns, a 17th century shaft and a mediaeval cross-head found at the time.

Inspired by the 1910 excavations, John Henry Cooke, the Town Clerk, set out to write the history of Vale Royal, then turned that into a rather dreary and poor gothic novel. Much of his valuable research is included but it becomes difficult to separate fact from fantasy. He claims to have found the name Ida on the base of the cross (*ie* on a column base only put there in 1813) but the writer has never traced it. Similarly his claim to have found a book belonging to Ida is fiction.

The basic story is that Ida, a young girl from Overton, was befriended by Peter, a Canon of Norton Priory. He became Abbot of Vale Royal (an unlikely change of monastic order!) and she entered the Convent of St Mary at Chester. The Abbot had to visit the city and was taken ill but was nursed back to health by Ida and they fell in love. They realised that their vows prevented any relationship on earth, but agreed to be buried in the same grave to be together for eternity. The likelihood of such an arrangement is remote and permission for such a burial impossible to obtain. The 19th century OS map on which Cooke claims to have found the name Nun's Grave actually says 'Nunsgreave', not grave. Much of the fiction in the book is nonsense, especially the involvement of the Devil and the legend of Over Church, and this sadly detracts from Cooke's undoubted antiquarian achievements.

Vale Royal Abbey, by Basil Pendleton, based on the 1910-11 excavations. The east end was not explored and is not shown. It resembles Nantwich Church and the same masons are believed to have worked on both.

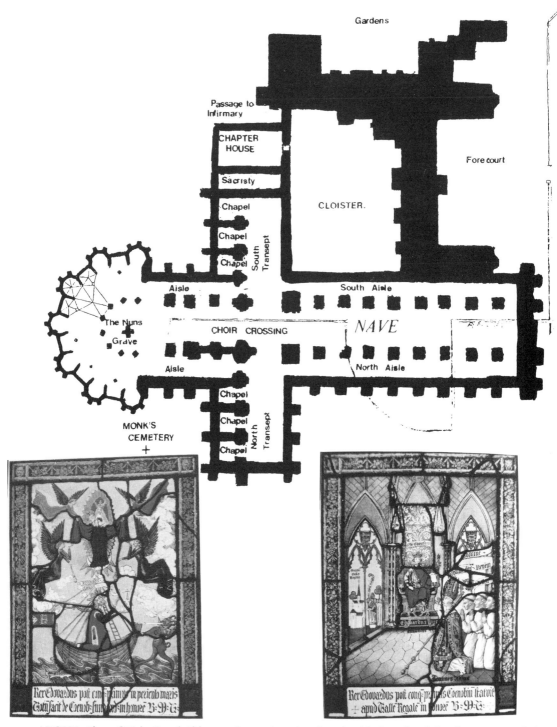

ABOVE: Plan of Vale Royal Abbey and mansion showing the 13 chapels of the chevet around the altar. (GC) BELOW LEFT: The vow of Prince Edward to found the Abbey. He is offering a model of it to the Virgin – from a stained glass panel formerly at Vale Royal, and RIGHT: Edward commands Abbot John and the monks to establish the Abbey, which can be seen through the window.

Monastery and Mayhem

Perhaps the most spectacular single event in Winsford's history was the ceremony on 13 August 1277, when King Edward I, his Queen Eleanor and their courtiers, came to lay the foundation stones of the Abbey high altar at Vale Royal. He had vowed to found the Abbey while in danger of shipwreck crossing the Channel. Now he was about to embark upon an invasion of North Wales and this act of piety was a prelude to the building of the Welsh Castles, in which builders from Vale Royal were involved. His Chancellor, Burnell, Bishop of Bath and Wells, was present, but the honour of conducting the service was given to Anian, Bishop of St Asaph, who had invited Edward to invade his diocese to restore order. The King set out on the invasion as soon as he left Vale Royal, no doubt feeling assured of heavenly help.

A silver chalice and paten (now in the National Museum of Wales) were discovered at Dollgellau in Wales in 1890. An inscription recorded it was made for 'Walter out of Hereford'. Walter was the name of the second Abbot of Vale Royal and the monks had moved from Abbey Dore in Herefordshire, where they had befriended the Prince in his captivity during the Baron's War. It has been conjectured that Walter gave the plate for use at the foundation service. Confusingly the first master mason was also known as Walter de Hereford. It is known that the King collected the silver seals of the defeated Welsh nobles and had them melted into a chalice for use at Vale Royal – was this the chalice?

The monks had petitioned the King that, at a spot called 'Holy Wheat' or 'Monk's Wood', 'Catholic and thoroughly trustworthy men' had seen visions of the Virgin on her feast days. This they claimed was a divine sign of where the Abbey should be built. Modern opinion, based on an early 17th century estate map of Vale Royal, now at Winnington Hall, suggests that the Abbey was built near the site of the village of Conersley, from which tenants were moved. It is mentioned in Domesday Book, but vanishes from the records after the Abbey was founded. The estate map shows the name for fields to the west of the house. Geophysical surveys in 1995 failed to find a trace, but this is not conclusive, as it might have been just outside the area surveyed.

Seven stone crosses are recorded: at Darnhall School Green, St Chad's Drive, Over Square, Salterswall, Marton Grange and Marton Beeches. The bases remain at Salterswall and Marton. These may mark spots where the procession of sacred relics rested on their way from Darnhall to Vale Royal or they may have been boundary markers for the forest of Mara.

John Henry Cooke named his house 'Crossfield' because he walked across the fields to get to it. Some writers have suggested that there was a cross there too, but Cooke never mentions it in *Ida*, and Crossfield is not recorded as an ancient field name.

The Abbey was intended to be 'the finest and fairest Cistercian house in the land' and to house 100 monks. Yet, it was never completed and seldom housed more than 20. Edward lost interest as North Wales was subdued. The building of castles, rebuilding of Chester walls and castle and the work at Vale Royal were the largest building operations undertaken by any mediaeval monarch in Europe. It left the Royal coffers exhausted and the King's interest had anyway moved on to the 'hammering of the Scots'.

The original church, at 420ft long, was the largest Cistercian church in England and, if the original plan had been carried through, this would have been one of the finest abbeys in Christendom. Vale Royal was always under-endowed and impoverished. Complaints were made about the cost of hosting the wealthy visitors with horses and dogs for whom the Abbot had to provide suitable accommodation. After Edward withdrew support they had to struggle to complete their Abbey church with little more than the revenue of their limited estates. The church was finally completed by the Black Prince who commissioned a continental-style arrangement of chapels known as a chevet at the east end in 1358. He had visited the Abbey the year before. The Abbey needed many chapels to allow every monk and visiting priest to say his daily masses in front of an appropriate altar. The living quarters may never have been properly completed in stone. Recent surveys have shown that much mediaeval timber-framed structure remains cased in later stonework in the south and west wings. These may have been the refectory, kitchen, lay brothers' quarters and Abbot's residence, completed in timber-frame to save money.

It was recorded in the Abbey journal that, when completed, men had come to the aid of the church when it glowed as if on fire. This might be explained by the red of a sunset shining on the huge decorated windows, with their wide pointed arches filled with stained glass.

It is strange that the vast church was built before the choir, especially as the foundation stone of the high altar was laid first. No sign of a temporary cover of stone or timber frame was observed in 1958. Yet it is unthinkable that the altar would have been left exposed to the weather for over 60 years. It was usual to begin at the east so that services could start under cover as soon as possible.

In 1360 a great gale demolished the central tower, which fell and destroyed the nave – 'The columns fell like trees'. There can be little doubt that the vast structure was just too heavy for its foundations on sandy clay. The Black Prince's work was not affected and excavations showed that that work was completed.

There was no further Royal patronage, though Richard II gave permission for a much smaller church to be built. The only other Royal event was the visit of Henry VII with Queen Elizabeth in 1495. They were on the way to a grand reception at Latham Hall in Lancashire given by John Stanley, Lord Derby, who was responsible for Henry's victory at Bosworth Field. Abbot John Buckley later served in person on the Royal side at the battle of Flodden with many of his tenants.

Unrest and dissatisfaction were evident for many years. In 1320 a servant of the Abbey, John de Bodeworth, was set upon by the Oldynton brothers, (recorded elsewhere as landowners). They cut off his head and kicked it. One of the skeletons found in 1958 was headless, but a skull was found near the base of a nearby pillar as if buried separately out of reverence. There was no sign of identity.

Brother John Lewis was also set upon when returning from Chester. He was forced to take shelter, in fear of his life, at the house of Simon Blaby. A rebellion of 1329, just before the Abbey was officially opened, suggests that the monks were more than usually keen on collecting every farthing due to them. Those involved were tried and were taken away with halters around their necks.

Our knowledge of these matters is one-sided since it comes solely from the Abbey Ledger Book. Customs included being forced to stand guard at Darnhall Tower whenever guards were mounted at Chester, no freedom to marry outside the village, use of the Abbot's mill without choice, and the Abbot's right to a man's possessions and livestock (right down to bees!) on his death.

In 1336 things must have become intolerable. Men from Over and Darnhall stopped the Justiciar of Chester at Herbache Cross (the boundary of Cuddington with the forest). They claimed that, although they were free men, the Abbot treated them as villeins. When they returned, the Abbot ordered them to be confined in fetters until they admitted their bondage. Some decided to take the matter to a higher level and set off on the pretext of a pilgrimage to the shrine of St Thomas of Hereford. They traced the King but, after waiting for several days, were thrown into Nottingham jail because of misconduct. The King heard of their plight and ordered them to be freed. They went to Westminster to plead their case, saying that they were too afraid to return home.

The King ordered the Justiciar of Chester to investigate, but the Abbot held all the records, including (presumably) the charter of Over, which he might have withheld. The Justiciar sided with the Abbot, ordering him to punish the men. They next petitioned Queen Philippa, claiming that they were tenants of her son as Earl of Chester, not of the Abbot. She wrote to the Abbot ordering him to cease persecuting them and threatening to tell the King. He took his answer in person to the King, to avoid Royal displeasure. The King ordered the documents to be examined. The illiterate peasants had no ammunition against them.

As the Abbot was returning through Rutland he was set upon and his servant William Fynche was shot with an arrow. The Abbot escaped and the three ringleaders went into hiding. When they were eventually captured they were put in the stocks at Weaverham, then forced to swear that they were bondsmen, and were ordered to stand bareheaded and barefooted for many Sundays in full view of the congregation in the Abbey.

Abbot Peter might have won the case but he was eventually assassinated. It seems incredible that John Henry Cooke should have chosen Peter, above all people, to portray as a kindly hero in his fanciful novel *Ida*.

LEFT: A Cistercian monk in white habit; men like this inhabited Vale Royal. ABOVE: The coat of arms of Vale Royal Abbey includes the Royal Standard. RIGHT: The crosshead of the Nun's Grave, set up in 1813, with the mediaeval carving of St Nicholas, one of the Abbey patrons. (NAG)

ABOVE: View from the site of the Abbey altar in 1774 showing the cloister wall retained as a walled garden. Note the quantity of timber work, showing that the domestic part of the Abbey used local timber frame. BELOW: The remnants of the Nun's Grave in 1990, showing the same view as the previous one of the house. The circles on the pillar base stones held shafts of Purbeck marble. (C)

ABOVE: Over Fair at the turn of the century, showing temporary stalls set up on Delamere Street outside the Black Bear. (C) BELOW: Delamere Street in the 1900s at the heart of the old borough. The wheelwright to the left is already advertising as a 'cycle shop and remained as one until the 1970s. Several timber-framed thatched cottages show how picturesque it was.

An Ancient Borough

A charter c1280 granted by the Abbot and confirmed by the King, created a free borough of Over. This gave the burgesses the right to dig turves for burning from the bog on Blakeden Moss and the use of the north well. They had to maintain a pillory and prison. They were granted market rights and forbidden to sell at any other. Rent was set at 12d for each burgess twice a year. The role of Abbot's Seneschal evolved into that of Mayor. This was part of the consolidation of Cheshire as a sound market centre to serve invasion troops in North Wales. Several other Cheshire towns gained borough status around that time.

Over parish was always a collection of small groups of houses (as it remained until the present century), each with their own open fields and identity. Whitegate, Little Budworth, Wettenhall and St John's parishes have been created from what was an extensive parish. Domesday Book records that in Saxon times Over was held as four manors and the older four parishes could be related to those manors.

There is no supporting evidence that the church was at the centre of a Saxon village which 'drifted away'. This idea was based on outdated ideas about deserted villages. The valley is not suited for houses and aerial photographs have never revealed anything. Housing would have tended to follow the line of Swanlow Lane, forming the settlement of Churton.

Parish, manor, borough, estate and township are all different administrative terms. One is religious, two relate to administration and two to land ownership. There is no reason at all why they should refer to the same area. The borough and manor were much smaller than the parish. The manor house was one of the few buildings to keep company with St Chad's after the Reformation. It related to the time when the manor was owned by Edmund Purshall, a London merchant, who presented armorial silver to the church. Purshall purchased the right to appoint the Vicars of Over and Whitegate along with those of numerous other parishes. They in turn paid annual fees to keep their appointment. He became bankrupt and the manor was sold to Thomas Cholmondeley in 1737.

The church is the parish, and not the borough, church. In such a vast parish it must have been inconvenient for most parishioners no matter where the church was built, yet Over must have the most awkwardly sited church in relationship to its parish, for it is only yards from the boundary. Church and borough were founded some 500 years apart, under different conditions. It was normal in Cheshire for a completely separate market town to develop within large parishes, as Northwich did in Great Budworth and Nantwich in Acton.

Examination of the first edition Ordnance Survey map shows a grouping of houses on Delamere Street, planned as a small mediaeval borough. The inhabitants, known as burgesses, each had a house set in a burgage plot, for which they were to pay 12d twice a year. Beyond this were the croft and toft, enclosures for growing vegetables and keeping livestock. All were retained within back lanes (which still exist as Moss Bank and Whitby's Lane) for delivery of harvest and animal access. This is typical mediaeval planning and, in rural areas particularly, the main door of the old property is often at the back.

The Abbot was in the embarrassing position of being lord of the manor, while the parish church belonged to another house. The loyalty of the incumbent to him was by no means assured. In 1437 Vicar Richard de Asthull and a group of men killed Abbot Henry de Weryngton in Bradford Wood, as he was attempting to abduct Mary Hector of Over.

The natural site for a market place would seem to be the wide area at the entrance to the church yard, but this was alien territory to the Abbot. The nuns gave up their land in Over to the Abbey in exchange for an annual rent. In Victorian times the market and horse fair were both held in Delamere Street, where a market hall was built around 1840. Mayor-making dinners and courts were traditionally held in the George and Dragon. The Abbot's borough was probably this limited area on Delamere Street, which remained part of the Vale Royal Estate until 1912.

There is ample evidence in the number of timber-framed cottages, often covered with a later brick facing, to show that Over was involved in what has been described as 'the Great Rebuilding'. In the 17th century methods of house building changed, from using insubstantial materials which did not last more than a generation or two, to solid construction which lasted for centuries. The number of similar cottages recorded in old photographs and still surviving shows Over could have been one of the prettiest timbered villages in the county.

Between borough and church were the Town Fields, or more properly *ton* (settlement) fields, as Over never became a town. The name is used for two streets, and the ridge and furrow of strip farming can be seen around St Chad's. They show, extending west of Swanlow Lane, on aerial photos taken before the town's modern expansion. They can be seen from the road when the light is right, sweeping down to the west bank of the Flash. The long narrow gardens of Swanlow Lane indicate that each was a collection of strips. It is not possible to say which settlement owned which fields. Excellent views of the Wharton strips in the fields are visible from 'buses passing along Bostock Road.

Legend tried to explain the situation with the tale that the Devil stole the church from the town centre, intending to drop it on Nantwich Church. He was foiled by the monks, who remembered his aversion to bells and rang out the Abbey peal. The prayers of Over people ensured it rested safely in the valley, a mile from the original site.

Apparently the Abbot established the borough firmly on his own land. There seems to have been some response, in that a rival chartered borough at a place called Murfield, in Over, was mentioned in a document of 1330. The location is unknown and the name is lost. Competition between the two may have caused both to falter. The second market's failure has also been attributed to the nearby market at Middlewich and to the disruption caused by the Black Death. However, a revived Over market and fair continues to be held as the charter instructed.

The local rebellion of 1366 shows that the Abbot was not respecting the borough status of his tenants as free men. Vale Royal was always desperately short of money, as insufficient land had been granted. The rebellion was probably triggered by increasing pressure on tenants to cover costs caused by gale damage six years earlier. The Black Death of 1349 would have reduced numbers paying rents and available builders.

The power of mayors has been overestimated. There is no proof that they had the power to issue the death sentence. A field name – 'Gallows Loont' – on Swanlow Lane, derives from the Saxon *gallas* (a piece of land) and *loont* (a ploughland). The Court House Farm further along Swanlow has been put forward as the site of the borough court, but this is too far from the borough, and could derive its name from other sources.

Over Cross in Delamere Street contains the lock-up where drunks and petty criminals were held overnight until the Mayor could attend to their cases. It appears to date from around 1840 when the market was revived. It is a unique structure, though the base of the mediaeval cross at Deeping St James, Lincolnshire, also contains a lock-up. A small excavation between it and the 17th century cottage which was once by its side unearthed a boundary ditch. The pottery from that was of 17th/18th century date and the ditch ran right under the cross, proving that it was built comparatively recently.

The market hall had been built by private subscription for £500, but Lord Delamere purchased it to convert it to a school. It was struggling to compete with the old Winsford Market Hall in the Market Place and, as Delamere had obtained the market rights there too, the decision was not entirely philanthropic!

Over never developed beyond village size and the mayors were often mocked for being simple working men. In the 17th century the saying 'The Mayor of Altrincham and the Mayor of Over, one's a thatcher t'other's a dauber' (plasterer) is first recorded. A tale with a similar theme tells that a mayor went to Altrincham to meet their mayor. When he arrived in the town he spotted a barber's and decided to clean up. He told the barber that he could tell his customers he had been given the honour of shaving the Mayor of Over. Unimpressed, the man replied that he could tell the people of Over that he had been shaved by the Mayor of Altrincham.

The Mayor was ranked second only to the Mayor of Chester in importance but it was said:

'For honours great and profits small,
The Mayor of Over beats them all'.

The origin of the tale that the Mayor had the right to disturb the middle one of any three pigs and lie down in its place – if the other two did not object! – is unknown.

In the 19th century the court of the lord of the manor was held each October in the George and Dragon. The present building has a large upstairs room designed for such meetings. Two juries were empanelled, one called the Grand Jury for the borough and the other the County Jury for the country areas. Six names were put forward annually to Lord Delamere by the Grand Jury. One of these was nominated Mayor at a meeting held 14 days later. During the year he assumed the role of JP for Over, Marton and Swanlow. Licences for inns and public houses were signed by him, along with the County magistrates, and at the quarter sessions he took his seat with them on the bench. This was probably the cause of the jokes since JPs at the time were land-owning gentlemen.In later days it was usually a prosperous farmer who took the office and it was regarded as a mark of status to have been Mayor. After serving they were entitled to be known as Aldermen.

The Vale Royal estate books record annual payments to Thomas Thomlinson, the landlord, for Jurymen's dinners at the annual Mayor-making courts. Lord Delamere always paid the bill, which was £5 10s 0d in 1842.

The fairs were known as 'cabbage' on 15-17 May and 'onion' on 25-27 October. A cattle fair, at which Christmas poultry was also sold, was held from 9-11 December. The Mayor and officials met at the cross and 'walked the fair', preceded by the mace to clear the way. They went then for a meal at one of the seven inns in Delamere Street.

Elections were not always taken as seriously as today and the following was posted in Over in 1882:

'FELLOW RATEPAYERS: Having been asked by a large and influential body (as was shown by the votes accorded to me at the meeting the other night) and being nominated by a desire to get as near to the top of the tree as possible: also feeling that I should not be backwards in coming forward, I earnestly solicit your votes. (Although I know I shall have plenty without them) in the pending election of which, I with my friend "TEDDY" have been the sole cause. My rival "Charles", the oldest established and only practical auctioneer in the place, tried to fight hard to fight shy of a contest for he knows he has no chance as long as we are patted on the back by "THE LADY KILLING ALDERMAN" and his Chief "THE PARSON". Being a large land owner in Over and other parts of the Country, and having the support of the Darnhall Tenantry, I consider it your duty to elect me, as I am causing you to pay the expense of the election expenses. After giving you my word to abide by the decision of the meeting convened at the early part of the week and being a large payer of the Income Tax I am greatly interested in keeping the rates up, I mean down, I will keep present schoolmaster's salaries up as I might need a little help on that side myself sometime. Having given you an insight of what you may expect from me I leave the rest to your judgement, knowing what an ignorant class I have to deal with. Jan 32nd, 1882 Josef Bigtimber [Joseph Smallwood].'

The Local Government Act of 1894 took away the Mayor of Over's right to be a JP, but did not object to Over continuing to elect a mayor. It continued the ceremonial of mayor-making and the inspection of the fair by the Mayor each year. The court appointed ale-tasters, (one for Over and one for the country), burleymen, who settled small disputes, and constables. The livestock fair closed down, with Government restrictions on cattle trading in streets, and insistence on regular cattle markets which could be inspected.

Over was recognised as the smallest municipality in the country in 1894. Edmund Leigh was the last Mayor, who died just two years later, bringing the independent office to an end. In 1899 an attempt was made to revive the Court Leet with J. E. Reiss of Cassia elected Mayor, but this did not last long. The first meeting after reorganisation took on something of the role of an amenity group. They agreed to pressure the Urban District to provide seats on which walkers might rest. Walking was not only the way most people got about but a popular leisure activity and one of the precious few allowed on a Sunday.

When it was proposed to end the tradition where the owner of Vale Royal, as Lord of the Manor, appointed the Mayor, Lord Delamere did not agree. It was intended to pass the title in an honorary capacity to the Chairman of the UDC. Delamere hit the table at the George and Dragon with the mace (the dent can still be seen) to drive home his point. He took the damaged mace, which his ancestor had donated, back to Vale Royal. Later, it was privately purchased and returned when the estate was disposed of shortly after the Second World War. The mace has the arms of Thomas Cholmondeley and his two wives along with the arms of William and Mary, but also the rose and crown emblems of Jacobite supporters of the exiled James II. Sir John Brunner presented a new mace for the Chairman to mark the Coronation of 1910. It was topped with the Prince of Wales' coronet, a reminder that the eldest son of the monarch is the Earl of Chester as a result of the death of the last Norman Earl at Darnhall. It is probably unique in that respect. Now the Mayor of Winsford is preceded by both the Over, and Winsford maces, a rare distinction. The *ex-officio* title, Mayor of Over was last used in 1974.

ABOVE: Chairman and Mayor of Over, Cllr Wilf Forgham, with Seneschals on the way to a factory opening in the '60s, preceded by the two maces. (WTC) LEFT: The Winsford Mace (1910) with the Prince of Wales' coronet and RIGHT: the 17th century Over Mace. The old one has the arms of William and Mary in the crown, but also has the rose and crown of the Jacobite followers of the exiled James I – hedging bets.

ABOVE: The George and Dragon still has the large assembly room upstairs where the Court Leet met to elect the Mayor. (C) BELOW: The old Smithy in Over, where Saxon Crossway is today, from the Delamere Sales Book of 1912. (TS)

36

ABOVE: Over Brewery and thatched house, Delamere Street, 1912.
(TS) BELOW: School Farm by St John's School; one of several in the
town which faced the main roads. (TS)

ABOVE: One of several lead spindle whorls used in 14th century textile production, found in Over – actual size. (MM) LEFT: The legend of Over Church from Egerton Leigh's *Cheshire Ballads and Legends*. RIGHT: The stump of the Calvary cross, the tower, porch parvise (priest's room) and one of the windows of Starkey's south aisle. The Good Friday service was preached from the steps of the cross in the Middle Ages. (C) BELOW: This aerial view of St Chad's shows remnants of the formerly circular churchyard – a sign of an early foundation. (NAG)

ABOVE: The brass of Hugh Starkey on the right should date from around 1540-50 but is almost identical in the style of armour and details to the Delves brass at Wybunbury church and dated 1515. BELOW: One of Winsford's hidden treasures, St Chad's church, with the rebuilt Bluebell Inn, where parishioners could get refreshment after long services before travelling several miles home. (C)

ABOVE: 'The deer's clearing' – the moat at Darley Hall Farm once surrounded Hugh Starkey's 16th century house. (NAG) BELOW: Marton Grange (here in 1816) was demolished in 1840 but the bridge, containing remnants of the drawbridge over the moat, remains.

Rooms for Improvement

Land-ownership changed dramatically in the Tudor period with the Dissolution of the Monasteries in 1536. The Abbot went to London claiming that he had not agreed to give up the Abbey and the document which he was said to have signed was a forgery. Nonetheless, Vale Royal passed to Thomas Holcroft, who had been instrumental in the closure, and was possibly linked to the forgery. This fulfilled a prophecy by Robert Nixon that 'yon house a raven's nest shall be'. Holcroft's crest was a raven. He purchased the Abbey and all its estates, from Swanlow to Weaverham, for the bargain price of £450 10s 6d in 1543. The Abbey buildings cost another £464 10s 0d. He proceeded to convert the monastic buildings to a huge H-plan, representing his initial.

Whitegate Church had served as parish church for the Abbey tenants, at the gate to the precinct. Resistance against returning to Over parish was evident and a petition was presented to Henry VIII. Parishioners claimed that 'before the time of remembrance of man' they had been a separate parish but that Papal documents had been destroyed at the Dissolution. If they were returned to Over, hardships such as fees charged by the Vicar and customs, whereby they would even have to pay to marry out of the parish, would ruin their lives. Henry created Whitegate parish in 1542. The choir wear red cassocks even to this day in recognition of that Royal foundation. Some writers have attributed the timber columns to the Middle Ages. Examination shows them to be too straight and slender when compared with genuine work at Lower Peover or Warburton. They resemble boat masts and may have had their origins in a Victorian boat yard on the Weaver.

Holcroft demolished the Abbey church so that not a single stone remains above ground. Excavations by Basil Pendleton in 1911-12 proved the existence of a cruciform church. The 12 chapels arranged in a semicircle around the altar, which the Black Prince had agreed to build, were traced by F. H. Thompson in 1958.

In 1615 the Holcroft house was purchased by Lady Mary Cholmondeley, the heiress of the Holfords of Plumley. She was establishing a new dynasty, having married into the richest family in the county. In 1616 she entertained James I and his court on his famous journey around the north. It is said she declined an offer of a place at court for her sons so that the King dubbed her 'the Bolde Ladie of Cheshire'. An oak-panelled room was the one where she slept; later painted inscriptions recorded this and the stay of Henry VII. There was said to be a secret room where each heir was taken to face something which would change his life. No trace of the room and its fearful contents have been found in the recent restorations.

Lady Mary's post-mortem enquiry reveals that she died in 1630 owning the site of the dismantled Abbey, four cottages, two dovecotes, eight gardens, six orchards, six granges, free warren and the goods and chattels of felons and waifs and strays in Vale Royal, Weaverham, Over and Marton.

Hugh Starkey obtained Knight's Grange from Henry VIII and used the estates to expand his territory to become the owner of most of Over. He served as Gentleman Usher (a predecessor of Black Rod) to the King. He rebuilt the south wall and probably the tower of St Chad's in 1543. The mason's marks are the same as on the towers at Weaverham and Tattenhall. It formed an imposing funeral church for his family. The ancient east window was saved because it contained stained glass portraits of his grandparents. The impressive range of windows in the south wall was probably intended for more glass memorials. However, he only left daughters so the estate was split up.

Hugh Starkey's documents indicate the presence of looms, weavers and spinners in 16th century Knight's Grange. Other evidence of textile production includes over a dozen lead spindle whorls, found along the ridge and of mediaeval date. Some are in the Manchester Museum and others in the County Museums Service's care. There is ample mention of sheep farming in the Abbey accounts. A shepherd's house, now Keeper's Cottage and a substantial building, is shown next to Pettypool on the 1616 estate map. It indicates the important position of the shepherd and the number of sheep.

There are records of the presence of a tomb to Hugh Starkey and another to his father and mother, both topped by brass portraits. The present tomb has been moved from the side of the chancel steps when the church was extended. The black marble top and the quality of the brass is superior to the tomb, the inscription and the shields. Even allowing that the 'portrait' was purchased from stock, the difference of quality is striking and it lies uneasily to the rear of the tomb arch. Examination of the marble reveals that a brass inscription has been removed while the father's tomb is recorded as having an inscription around the edge.

One is forced to agree with the opinion of Rev Francis Powell, who believed that the brass of the father had been put onto the tomb of the son. A large tomb outside the east is argued to be the re-used tomb of the father. To support the theory the armour depicted is that of the time of Henry VII (as on the Delves tomb at Wybunbury), not of the period of Henry VIII. The tomb was erected during Starkey's life and the date was left blank to be filled in after he died. It was never completed. His only son, an illegitimate one, was serving as secretary to the Knights of St John of Malta and retained the Catholic faith. He served as secretary to the Grand Prior and recorded the siege of Malta by the Turks. The inscription starting 'of your charity pray for the soul' shows that it was set up under Catholic traditions. Yet that would not have been allowed at the time of his death in 1555.

The rebuilding also included Catholic features, with a decorated stoup for holy water in the porch. A piscina for washing sacred vessels is at the (former) east end of the south wall. The Starkey tomb to the left of the altar is designed to form an Easter sanctuary. The bread and wine consecrated on Good Friday would be kept there for use on Easter Sunday, representing Christ in the tomb. These features demonstrate that, although the King assumed supremacy in the Church of England, little changed in the way of worship until the reign of Edward VI. The stoup and churchyard cross shaft were broken by later Puritans and the cross shaft is topped by a sundial dated 1745. The registers started in 1558.

A strange document in Sir Peter Leycester's papers in the British Museum suggests that Marton Grange was leased by the Mainwaring family from Abbot John for a rent of £3 10s 0d. Ormerod dates this to 1539, but this must be an error as the Abbey was closed by then.

Lady Mary Cholmondeley probably built the brick mansion at Knight's Grange. This is one of the oldest brick buildings in the county. It would have looked most

42

impressive in the new material when it was completed. Excavations suggest the two moats date from this period. They both produced plenty of pottery etc thrown in as rubbish, but little earlier than the Tudor period. The pollen analysed from the Marton moat was predominantly grass pollen, suggesting that the forest had been cleared well before the moat was dug. A wooden tennis ball and bowling wood show that sport was enjoyed at 17th century Marton. Other moats in the district survive at Darley Hall, Oulton and at Bostock Old Hall; suspected moats were filled in near Wharton Bridge and at the Nun House in recent years.

The west room (parlour) at Knights contained one of the finest Jacobean fireplaces in the north-west. It did not survive conversion to a pub by the UDC in the 1970s. All that remains are two vernacular paintings from the overmantel in the care of the County Museums Service.

Darnhall was purchased with other Cheshire manors by Rowland Hill, a London merchant, for £682. Thomas Lee held the manor during the Civil War. His mother left him £200 to pay a schoolmaster to teach the youth and inhabitants of Darnhall and neighbourhood. Lee added to this with the help of six other Darnhall men to build a school at Jackson's Croft near to Holding Cross. Trustees were appointed and a farm at Tattenhall was purchased; its rent was used to maintain the school. The original timber-framed school stood to the north of Darnhall Knobs. These are former gate-post markers of the entrance to Darnhall Estate at the head of an avenue, said to have been made from bricks from the old school, but they look more or less contemporary with its founding. The name School Green still survives. (General Robert E. Lee, the General of the American Civil War, was a descendant of the Lee family of Darnhall.)

The school was set up with a Presbyterian outlook and taught nonconformists as well as Anglicans basic subjects, though Latin and Greek were available on request. Girls were not allowed to stay once they had mastered the basics of worship. Darnhall is a detached part of Whitegate parish but it was originally known as Over and Darnhall Free School. In 1818 it moved to the present site. As the trustees were all churchmen they moved it nearer to St Chad's and it became more involved with the church.

During the Civil War the village of Over was occupied in 1643 by Sir Thomas Aston's Protestant troops. The constables' accounts in the Public Record Office record claims made by most of the villagers, both for the cost of accommodating soldiers and for personal items, including bibles and items of clothing which they claim were stolen. Rev Francis E. Powell records that soldiers left rat poison wrapped up like sweets in the cottages for the children to eat.

The military went on to destroy the north wing of Vale Royal House. Tradition has it that they removed everything portable except one gold plate with the family arms, hidden in a secret drawer, and the children's pony, hidden behind panelling. A white cow with pink ears is said to have escaped and returned home, where its milk provided sustenance for the family. Aston was arrested on the Restoration and spent the rest of his life a prisoner.

An exciting modern find in Nixon Drive was a black cup containing silver coins, the latest of which was dated 1643, the date of the occupation, and evidently hidden. Declared treasure trove, it is now in Grosvenor Museum at Chester, the coroner's verdict being that it had been hidden during the unrest. A second local hoard was found near Gale Green and these silver half-crowns of the Restoration period were so fine they were purchased as treasure trove by the British Museum.

The late 17th century poem *The journey to the North of England by Drunken Barnaby* records that he:

'Came to Over o profane one,
And there he met a puritain one,
A hanging his cat on a Monday,
For killing a mouse on a Sunday'.

A survey of timber-framed buildings conducted in 1976 showed how they clustered along the ridge from Weaverham to Church Minshull. Most were attributed to the 17th century, apart from Littler Farm and Dalk House (Swanlow Lane). Littler has a timber wing with evidence that another timber-framed wing was replaced in brick. That dates from the 16th century and has heavy decorative timbers with jettied floors. Dalk House represents the latest phase of timber-framed work with proper chimneys. The entrance was in the usual place by the main fireplace and is dated 1711. It has a T-shaped plan with a room projecting to the north which has its own separate entrance and no link to the rest of the house. This indicates it was used as a dairy on the cold side of the house, as these were exempt from window tax when not connected to the house.

Most 17th century examples were originally of single floor construction with thatched roof and later bedrooms were inserted in the roof-space served by dormer (sleeping) windows. All were constructed on a box-frame construction with panels of wattle and daub; some were replaced by brick 'nogging' or even enclosed in a brick facing. The usual plan was a central house-place with an open hearth covered by a smoke hood and backed by a stone or brick wall. This heated during the day and after curfew acted like a radiator to warm the bedroom on the other side.

Sometimes a store room is included in the plan. Others formed laithe houses (as at Marton Beeches – now altered) where a barn and/or byre were included under the same roof line. Demolition of a cottage, formerly by Over Cross, showed marks cut into the timber to number every joint in Roman numerals. This showed how the house had been prepared at the carpenter's yard, then erected like a construction kit. Some of the timbers were re-used as partition walls in Knights Grange. Unusual Arabic letters can be seen on the cottage facing Whitegate school. The number of similar cottages surviving and known from old photos is further evidence of a general rebuild in the 17th century.

A few fine Georgian houses survived until the demolitions of the 1960s. These included Oak House, Over Lodge and Oaklands by Wharton Bridge and nicknamed Smoke Hall. Wharton House is believed to be by the same architect, but it lost all interest when the Regency white paint and veranda were removed in a recent misguided restoration. There is little surviving Georgian work apart from the old St Chad's Vicarage and the central part of Wharton Hall. This confirms other evidence of the small scale of Winsford's industrialisation before the 19th century, though any cottages of this period probably went in slum clearance.

Stanthorne Hall is a fine example of a Regency mansion on the edge of town, built in the first decades of the 19th century and still with its picturesque landscape, imitating a Claude painting. Tradition has it that this was Miss Havisham's House of *Great Expectations*. That story seems to originate in a house on the opposite side of the road, where two spinsters lived in the 19th century. Locals probably started it by saying they were just like Miss Havisham, and before long it was rumoured that they were indeed that formidable lady.

ABOVE: Knights Grange, the 17th century mansion, was formerly moated – 1912. (TS) LEFT: Lay brother in working habit; it was workers like this who were the 'knights' (young men) who lived at the Grange. RIGHT: The only piece of sculpture known to survive from the Abbey, the head of a saint in Purbeck marble at Marton Grange. (NAG)

ABOVE: The Wishing Seat, the base of the cross at the entrance to Marton Grange. (C) BELOW: Weaver Hall, south of Winsford. In the 15th century the male line failed, Henry VII gave the daughter to be ward to the first Earl of Derby, who married her to his second son, establishing the new line of Stanley of Weaver and Alderley.

ABOVE: The Crest of Thomas Holcroft who purchased Vale Royal at the Dissolution. The raven crest which fulfilled Nixon's prophecy may be seen. CENTRE: Drawing of Vale Royal from the 1617 estate map, and BELOW: as depicted by Ormerod in 1816.

ABOVE: Vale Royal from the air; the D-shaped enclosure is the Nun's Grave on the site of the Abbey Altar. (NAG) BELOW: The Salon in the middle of last century; the roof timbers remain from the Abbot's hall.

ABOVE: The estate agent's office once had a sign made from a packing case addressed 'Ngoro' (in Kenya) as Lord Delamere's possessions were shipped from here to Africa. BELOW: Over Cross with timber-framed cottages c1900. The cross was built as a market cross around 1840 when the market was revived in the present school building. INSET: Memorial to the third Baron Delamere, the pioneer of white settlement in Kenya. (C)

49

LEFT: The rear of Over cross shows the blocked door to the cell inside. The Great Reform Bill of 1832 outlawed stocks and pillories, ordering lock-ups to be provided instead. This unique structure was Over's response. (C) RIGHT: The Market Hall in Market Place, which took away the trade of Over Market, was built in the 1850s. Between the wars it was used for roller skating, becoming the Strand Ballroom and later Mr Smith's Club. It was demolished in 1975 for road widening. (WTC) BELOW: Like the bones of a huge animal, the 17th century timber-frame emerges from behind brick facings at Over Cross Cottages in 1972. Much of the timber is now re-used in Knight's Grange. (NAG)

ABOVE: Group of timber-framed cottages long vanished from Delamere Street. BELOW: Littler Farm, the oldest house in Winsford, dating from the 16th century. (NAG)

ABOVE: This cottage, formerly in Delamere Street, is typical of many timber-framed cottages in the area; split into three dwellings during the housing shortage of the 19th century, it was later covered with brickwork to protect decaying beams and given a corrugated iron roof. LEFT: Robert Nixon, the Palatine Prophet, gave his name to Nixon Drive on the Grange Estate. RIGHT: The Over hoard of silver coins dated 1643 was probably hidden when the Parliamentarian army garrisoned the town that year. It was found in Nixon Drive.

They Went by Water

The story of Winsford changed for good after 1721, when the Weaver Navigation Act was passed, allowing the river to be made navigable as far as Winsford Bridge. This was the origin of the salt town of Winsford. Settlement developed on either side of the old stone bridge, which was the limit of navigation. For the first time, the men on the boats talked of 'going to Winsford'. Early records indicate that goods imported to and transported from Winsford by land as far as Derby were more important than trade in salt from Winsford.

One side-effect of this was better draining of the river valley, which had previously been avoided as damp and likely to flood. This allowed its development for industry. The development of the Flashes, as a result of salt subsidence from 1800 beyond the bridge, helped to reduce the risk of flooding and served as a reservoir. High water was contained there, often preventing flooding further down. Victorian Winsford had mixed views on the Flashes. Obsolete salt barges were sunk in it in an attempt at landfill but it was a popular resort to which to walk for the afternoon when the weather was fine and it attracted day-trippers from miles around.

It is said that the barges arrived black with coal and left white with salt. The Weaver has the longest proportion of its length, from source to mouth, navigable for sea-going vessels, of any river in the world.

Four salt pans were working near the bridge when the Act was passed but other works soon followed. Thomas Patten was the first to develop salt works and barges to transport it. In 1744 Isaac Wood leased the business and became the leading salt proprietor in Winsford. He almost held a monopoly of the trade on this part of the river until he died in 1782, when his widow took over. Besides salt he traded in pig iron, pottery, pipe clay, stone etc. He lived in the three-storey Oak House, on the highest point in Winsford, overlooking the valley from what is now Beeston Drive.

An unexpected feature of the Weaver Valley at that time was a furnace used for smelting iron. It was easier to transport large sheets of iron for pan-making locally by river and to use packhorses to bring small lumps of ore from the mining districts. After the Navigation, ore could come direct by water. It became the property of Abraham Darby, the celebrated ironmaster of Coalbrookdale in 1720. He identified the possibilities when the Navigation Act was proposed in Parliament.

The furnace is referred to as Vale Royal, but it is unlikely to have been near the house. Observation of the valley and maps lead to the conclusion that it could have been near the viaduct (which would have destroyed any trace). There the river bank is steep enough for loading ore and fuel at the top and molten iron to be taken from the bottom of the bank. Small brooks there could be harnessed to drive blast bellows. The monks had a bloomery (furnace) before this, though the size and location of their operation is not known.

The valley bottom was ideal for brine pumping. By the middle of the following century the river was lined with large salt pans from Winsford Bridge to New Bridge. Wild brine was pumped from the top bed of salt. This made Mid-Cheshire's salt trade more profitable and killed the Mersey industry. As the salt works prospered the areas where water entered the beds to become brine were eroding the salt.

This caused collapses, forming the Flashes. Other dramatic collapses occurred, such as the Ocean, Marton Hole and Sixes Hole – named after the owner of a cottage which was flooded by the sinking.

In the early years rock-salt for export to works on the Mersey was most profitable. There Lancashire coal was used and the rock salt was mixed with salty tide water to produce brine for boiling. This delayed development at Winsford where mines usually flooded. After the digging of the Sankey Brook Canal in 1757, coal could be shipped directly to the works and the same barges took the salt to Liverpool.

Unfortunately also in 1757 the collapse of the Northwich Lock into a salt mine, just upstream from Town Bridge, restricted Winsford's trade, for it took 21 months to repair and during all that time goods had to be transported by land around it, adding to costs. Isaac Wood unsuccessfully claimed compensation but Winsford's trade was severely hindered. A plan to dig an alternative canal from Winsford through Middlewich to Wrinehil in Staffordshire came to nothing.

In 1766 the construction of the Trent and Mersey Canal passed through Middlewich, revitalising that town. It was kept away from the salt-making towns of Winsford and Northwich by resistance from the Weaver Navigation Trustees. They did not want any threat to their monopoly of trade on the river or water supplies being diverted into the canal. The Weaver Navigation Act had been eased through Parliament by promises of an extension to Nantwich and to Middlewich, using the Dane. This stopped protests from the old salt towns, though neither was constructed, but plans for the Nantwich extension were revived as recently as 1951.

A new road was provided in 1784 as a link for Middlewich salt works *via* Gravel Hill (named because of the road surface), now known as Station Road. Intended for cart use, it diverted traffic from the old river crossing to the Winsford loading stages, in an attempt to attract cargo from the Trent and Mersey. This road became a turnpike in 1822 and later provided access for the town to Sandbach Station on the Manchester line.

Attempts to improve trade on the Weaver included deepening the channel and improving the locks in 1830. In 1860 the locks were improved and reduced in number. In 1870 new stone-lined locks were built by Edward Leader Williams, the Navigation Surveyor. They consisted of two chambers which held a single steam boat or four barges on each side. A steam boat could thus pull four 'dumb barges' behind it. The work was so impressive that it secured Leader Williams the job of designing the Manchester Ship Canal. Little traffic comes down the river to Winsford today, and silting has made it impossible for large craft to pass Northwich. The massive locks at Vale Royal are a memorial to a bygone era of trade and prosperity.

Winsford's six boatbuilding yards have all closed down, but an industry originating on the river still thrives. Sailmakers turned their talents in canvas work to develop the marquee business of Munton and Byron.

Similar resistance saw the railway kept a mile away from Winsford when it was built in 1837. Winsford Station is just as convenient for Middlewich, while Northwich is served by Hartford two miles away. The viaduct, designed by George Stephenson, had to be erected at the point where the gradient of the valley made loading salt onto trains impossible, and as far from the salt works as possible. Ideas of building the junction at Wharton were soon rejected by local landowners and it was moved to

Crewe, where a new town developed around it. Hartford Station prompted the development of a middle-class settlement but no such development took place in Winsford.

A branch line from the North Western Railway came to the Over and Wharton station at the top of Wharton Hill in 1870. Some of the original stone sleepers from the main line were used to build a retaining wall on Wharton Hill. A small section remains opposite the Top House pub, formerly called the North Western after the railway. A branch from the Cheshire Lines was constructed. It took freight and passenger trains to the end of New Road by the Navigation pub. It was one of the first lines dismantled after nationalisation. Though freight had been fairly consistent, several attempts to use it for passengers were not successful, especially after competition from 'buses arrived. Today the line of the track is preserved as the Whitegate Way country walk-way.

It is significant that, until the present century, there was no road leading to the salt works; the finished product left by boat and the men walked along the tow-path. New Road is now the main route to the salt mine, which produces 10,000 tonnes a week, or the equivalent of 850 tipper vehicle loads.

Heavy traffic to the salt mine was caused when the 'big freeze' of 1962 created a nation-wide demand for rock-salt. Lorries backed up , one behind the other, from the mine right up Wharton Hill and crept along at a slow pace. The weight, combined with erosive action of the wheels and expansion of moisture in the ground when it turned to ice, caused the road surface to crumble when the thaw arrived. A stockpile and depôt were then opened by the disused station. Salt could be dispatched avoiding traffic going direct to the mine. Road development in 1996 wiped away all traces of the station and most of the branch line.

Today Winsford has efficient trunk roads, which take traffic through without disrupting daily activities. In 1997 a new major link road joins up with the main Chester-Manchester road with easy access *via* dual carriageway to the M6. This has eased transport difficulties from the industrial estates which previously had to contend with little more than country roads, laid out for horsedrawn traffic and not lorries.

Winsford is also convenient for Manchester International Airport. Overflying is bound to increase with the construction of the second runway but Winsford is close enough to benefit.

ABOVE: Salt flatboats tied-up at Crosses Dock Yard, behind the old Town Hall and the Co-op café. Note the rowing boats from the Flash in the foreground. BELOW: Salt flats line the river at Meadow Bank around 1900 with the salt works behind. (CM)

ABOVE: Loading the flat *Berlin* around 1900 which changed its name because of anti-German feelings in the First World War. (CM) BELOW: Launching the *Monarch* (sideways as it was longer than the river was wide) in 1896; she was the biggest vessel ever built in Winsford and the Weaver bed had to be lowered to get her under Hartford Bridge.

ABOVE: A steam train crosses George Stephenson's viaduct at Vale Royal, built in 1837, (C) and BELOW: another at the Cheshire Lines' Winsford and Over Station. (C)

The Bottom Flash photographed when the new High Street and second bridge were in construction. The squarish protrusions from each bank are the filled-in Victorian filter-beds. The Marina was excavated in the 1960s through the bank of cinders from the salt works, tipped there to contain the water and reduce the risk of floods.

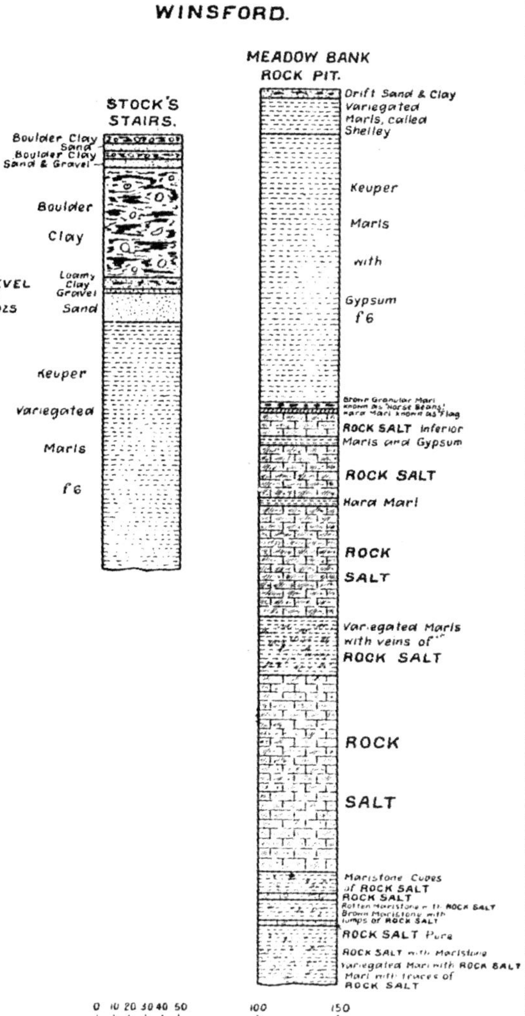

WINSFORD.

MEADOW BANK
ROCK PIT.

STOCK'S
STAIRS.

Boulder Clay
Sand
Boulder Clay
Sand & Gravel

Boulder

Clay

BRINE LEVEL
-37 50
£lbs 4½ozs

Loamy
Clay
Gravel
Sand

Keuper

Variegated

Marls

f6

Drift Sand & Clay
Variegated
Marls, called
Shelley

Keuper

Marls

with

Gypsum
f6

Brown Granular Marl
known as 'Horse Beans'
Hard Marl known as Flag
ROCK SALT Inferior
Marls and Gypsum

ROCK SALT

Hard Marl

ROCK

SALT

Variegated Marls
with veins of
ROCK SALT

ROCK

SALT

Marlstone Cubes
of ROCK SALT
ROCK SALT
Rotten Marlstone & ll ROCK SALT
Brown Marlstone with
lumps of ROCK SALT
ROCK SALT Pure
ROCK SALT with Marlstone
Variegated Marl with ROCK SALT
Marl with traces of
ROCK SALT

0 10 20 30 40 50   100   150

Scale of Feet

LEFT: Sections of the geology of Winsford from Calvert's *Salt in Cheshire*, 1915. RIGHT: Workmen standing by a brine pump around 1900. (CL)

Salt Sellers

Only one small salt house with four pans existed near Winsford Bridge when the Navigation Act was passed in 1721. During the 18th century the town struggled while Northwich held the supremacy in the salt trade, with less distance to carry salt and less obstacles. Difficulties such as the collapsed Northwich lock in 1757 added to Winsford's problems. Early production was limited to the flatter land on the Over side of the river and probably only utilised wild brine.

The salt production of the town remained almost a monopoly of Isaac Woods and the real growth of the town did not start until after 1796. This was a year after H. Wilkens, the first of a series of enterprising Germans, Dutch and Danes to hold key interests in the salt trade, joined the river transporters.

George Dudley (after whom East and West Dudley streets get their name) was prospecting on his land for brine. Almost ready to give up he sunk the final hole and struck a rich and powerful source. His men were hard pressed to escape unhurt from its force. He opened the first works in Winsford to use brine from boreholes and steam engines and started the equivalent of a gold rush.

Much of the land was in the hands of Thomas Cholmondeley of Vale Royal, who let out plots to prospectors on 50 year leases. These had the clause that, if no brine was found, they could be returned. Much of the early prospecting and the works that followed were undertaken by nonconformists. They entered into the project with the idea of not only making profits for themselves but of making work for idle hands. The migration from the countryside to the towns had started and there were plenty of willing hands to work in the salt sheds. The reduction of salt tax from £30 per ton to £4 in 1823 and its abandonment altogether in 1825 were the final incentive needed to make Winsford's industry viable.

This explains the rapid growth of Over and Wharton over the next 50 years and the fact that most places of worship can trace their origins back to those first decades of the 19th century.

By 1860, 500,000 tons of white salt were sent from Winsford along the Weaver. There were 416 salt pans (each with a smoking chimney), most of which were operating, employing upwards of 1,000 workmen. The number of women and children is not recorded, as they often worked for the man of the house, helping him. By the last part of the 19th century, Winsford was the largest salt-producing town in Britain, if not the world. However, foreign competition was starting to develop.

It is impractical to detail all the salt works, for Calvert recorded 297 individual salt proprietors by 1915 in Winsford alone. Many just worked for a year or two when prices were high and this increased competition, causing prices to fall and then the small traders closed down. It was their actions which helped accentuate the booms and busts of the Victorian era.

There was acute jealousy, the most vindictive probably that encountered by William Furnival. He patented a new method of using steam to crystallise salt. He claimed to make twice as much salt as from an ordinary pan of the same size and that his was superior. Threatening to cut the price of salt he came upon opposition from 'The Coalition', an association of salt manufacturers who agreed to keep prices artificially high to increase profits.

He opened a works in Wharton in 1828, which had over three miles of salt pans and produced 130,000 tons of salt a year; it cost £135,000 to build. He had ever-mounting debts from commercial adventures in the salt trade in this country and on the Continent and was arrested for debt in 1832. He is last heard of in London's Horsemonger Lane Gaol where he published his 'Statement of Facts', outlining his case and grievances.

The traditional method of making salt was to use large iron pans made from sheets of cast iron riveted together. Twenty-five feet was the optimum width for convenient working of the long rakes used to collect the salt. They could be of any length. The heat from furnaces at one end was fed, using brick channels, under the pans and into the adjoining 'hot house'. Wet salt was poured into elm wood tubs where it set like huge, block-shaped sand-castles. The blocks were dried in the hot houses and then ground to form white table or cooking salt. Much was packed in white cotton bags for export to Africa. It was used for barter in the slave trade before abolition and labels from closed-down works continued to be used because the natives recognised them as a sign of quality.

Groups of women from Winsford and Moulton were paid to sew up the bags on piece-work rates. To save time as they walked home they had strings cut to the right length tucked in their belts. A knot was tied on each one and it was passed to the other side ready for use the following morning.

Salt for domestic use was sometimes sold in large lumps for the cook to cut off as she needed. By the turn of 20th century the blocks of fine salt were being ground by machines and many young women were employed to pack it into cardboard cartons.

Coarse salt for cooking and industry was simply unloaded from the pans onto the 'hurdle' at the side. Fine salt was boiled quickly at a high temperature to make small crystals, the size controlled by careful timing. Coarse salts for fisheries and industry were heated slowly at a low temperature to create bigger crystals. It was loaded from the floors into two-wheeled hand carts and tipped directly into the hold of the barges and flats on the river. Vast wooden sheds supported by numerous columns existed on the bank of the river. They were built into the bank so that salt could be tipped in at roof/ground level and so keep vast stockpiles dry. It was unloaded from jetties overhanging the boats on the river. The last of these was near the bridge and demolished in 1996.

In the early years they served as bonded warehouses where salt could be stored without paying tax, which only became due when salt left. It was sensible to wait until the warehouse was reasonably full and then to transport it in bulk. The intention was to sell at once to obtain the money to pay the tax.

The conditions in the 19th century salt-works were notorious and Acts of Parliament aimed to improve them. Whole families would work on a co-operative basis and sleep in the works for most of the week. This helps to explain the apparent disparity between many salt works and little or inadequate housing in Wharton and Winsford shown on 19th century maps – even allowing that many workers came from Moulton, which developed from the 1830s. Sleeping in the works was considered acceptable when only one family was concerned, but immoral for more than one family to be together. Large numbers of children worked with their parents. As they did not appear on the payroll they were not subject to the normal regulations. Even small children helped with breaking salt-blocks and older ones with filling, sewing and moving bags.

Vagrants were allowed to warm themselves or to take a night's shelter in the works in exchange for labouring by the pans. This was frowned upon by works owners because so many people sleeping on the salt damaged it and reformers questioned its morality. Dangers included the chance of falling into the pans, which usually proved fatal. Falling with an arm in the brine stripped the skin and left the arm crippled. The introduction of a hand rail to catch hold of and prevent a fall only became standard between the wars. Men often chose to sleep by the stoke holes, where there was a risk of scalding from splashes of brine or burning from ashes falling from the fires. Women took babies to breast feed by the pans and would strip to undergarments in the heat. Men stripped to shorts and clogs and this was considered to promote lewd conduct. Many a middle-class visitor went to the salt works for the opportunity to observe this scant clothing rather than scientific interest in salt production. Wooden soled clogs were worn on the feet with pieces of sack called buskins, wrapped around the top to keep splashes of brine out. In 1872 Parliament forbade women and children to work by the pans and the Education Act made attendance at school compulsory in 1870 – though it was difficult to enforce.

The salt works closed on Mondays for the pans to be scraped clean and the women took the opportunity in the clean air to do the washing and drying. In 1868, a great strike for better pay and conditions was called throughout the whole district. Lost income from women and children was never properly compensated.

Herman E. Falk, a German works owner, by-passed strikes by importing, first German and then Polish, workers who were experienced in the industry. He recruited them from Liverpool, where they were awaiting emigration, with promises of steady pay. Winsfordians tell how they arrived with a luggage label on their lapel to indicate their destination. Unable to speak English the 'blacklegs' were shunned in the town and refused service in shops and pubs. He was criticised for the conditions in which they lived, but pointed out he merely let the property to a member of the community who sub-let as he wished.

Falk gives the impression of divided views. He was ruthless in his business enterprises but showed a benevolent face too. He organised a friendly society for his workers and built the famous bass houses for them. They were experimental in nature, using the clinker 'bass' which was a residue from the cheap, poor-quality coal used in the works. He also built a school in bass, paying for the master and mistress until it was taken over by the Over School Board. The door and window openings were of normal brick but the walls were of basses and were reported to be warm. Bass is hardly seen today but a sample remains in the retaining wall around the extension to St John's churchyard. One street of bass houses contained 28 interrelated families.

Falk had broken the power of the Flatmen's Friendly Society – one of the first trade unions who controlled prices for carrying salt. He introduced the first iron steam barges on the river. These arrived from 1863. They were named to represent the state of the trade: *Experiment, Development, Improvement* and *Supplement*.

In 1888 he was the most active of those who ensured that the Salt Union was formed, putting 90% of the industry into one company. It was the last of a series of groupings aimed at keeping salt prices high and steady. They also took control of the

Weaver fleet of barges. The idea was that all the salt works would combine into one company and, as all the former owners became share-holders in the new company, they would continue to receive a portion of the profits. This would allow small, inconvenient and unprofitable works to close and concentrate production in a few efficient factories. Redundancies and unemployment for the workers was bound to be one result.

The Union was not the success predicted. At first it had titled directors who had no experience of salt making. They paid more than the value for the works they purchased and failed to close the inefficient ones. Rather than sell at a reasonable price they felt their near monopoly of the industry would allow them to charge high prices. Independent producers simply under-priced them, Garner's and Hamlett's being the chief such firms in Winsford. By the end of the century salt-making profits had fallen to an all-time low.

In 1888 Sir John Brunner of the Winnington chemical works came to Winsford to address a mass meeting of salt workers, urging them to form a trade union to avoid persecution when the Salt Union was formed. The Winsford and District Salt Makers Association became a powerful force in the town and among other things it banned overtime!

The Salt Union introduced new conditions on the boats and the men claimed this gave them no time to sleep. The men struck in 1892, the year the salt mine closed. The Salt Union took the six ringleaders straight to court. The magistrates, sitting at Middlewich, were all Salt Union shareholders and the case was thrown out because they had been charged under a law which only applied to ships at sea. This, it was hoped, would defuse the situation.

The company employed men from out of town to do the work and, seeing this as a threat to their jobs, all the salt workers joined the strike. On 25 August a vessel called *Cynosure*, pulling a barge called *Antelope*, was showered with insults as it neared Northwich. The angry crowd followed it from the bank, shouting abuse until the engineer abandoned ship. The blacklegs were sent back to Liverpool.

Two days later a second boat with an escort of four police officers reached the outskirts of Northwich. Local police handed over to the Northwich force, who could not control the hundreds of jeering men and women who followed the vessel, showering it with bricks and stones. It was damaged and ran aground near Salterford Lock. The blackleg workers were sent back to Liverpool by train. Falk's executive vessel the *Nymph* was bombarded with bricks, so that officials had to have police protection to disembark and reach the offices.

The Winsford police force had to be augmented with a hundred officers from elsewhere in Cheshire. Most of the townsfolk assembled and the outsiders fled, leaving their bedding in the works where they were to sleep. Next day a train containing new labourers arrived at the Newbridge sidings, but they were met with such a violent and hostile crowd that they decided to return. Locals taunted them that they would not be able to survive in the heat and showed them the huge tools they had to use. Seventy officers escorted them out of the works. As they passed under an archway they were pelted with bricks and clinker, battering police helmets and cutting their faces.

The strikers stormed the Salt Union offices, throwing stones, but were driven back by officers with truncheons. Appeal was made to the Home Secretary for help and 100 Hussars were dispatched from Manchester.

The Mayor of Over, in his capacity as JP, threatened to read the Riot Act, but the crowd replied that it was the police who had started the riot. He appealed for them to disperse, which they did. The military remained on duty in the district, keeping the town under supervision. Eventually the dispute was settled by mediation by Dr Jayne, Bishop of Chester. Local men were forced to agree to pay £500 to reimburse the Liverpool men for their loss of wages.

The Union was never the monopoly that had been hoped, largely because of poor management and was absorbed by Brunner Mond in 1937. The name was revived when ICI sold the Winsford salt mine and its Runcorn salt works in 1992. The manufacturing of white salt in Winsford had ended. It was cheaper and more convenient to pump brine to Runcorn and operate works beside the ship canal, where the salt could then be exported directly by loading onto ships.

As late as the 1920s children at Moulton and Meadow Bank schools, with parents working in the salt works, were allowed out for an extra half hour at lunch time. They took ale and food to their parents. High Street Council Schools only let children out if they took the lunch box to school with them. Food was often heated by lowering it into the brine, and eggs boiled in brine were a common snack. Other items could be left in the brine to coat and Christmas trees 'frosted' with salt were popular. Children saw criminals marched from court past the saltworks to the Cheshire Lines station for transport to prison. They believed tales that they were taken to the salt works, stripped and flogged, before being dipped in brine to make the wounds sting. Brine was often applied to wounds as a crude anti-septic.

Changes were needed in the old methods of salt-making which used one ton of coal for every two tons of salt produced. In 1901 an experimental plant was built in the Island Works to try the new vacuum method, developed in America from sugar-refining plant. In 1906 the first full-scale plant started operation. The brine was heated in vacuum cylinders. Only one container is heated by freshly raised steam and so fuel consumption is much less. The steam from the first container heats the second and so on. Because the brine is heated in a vacuum, less energy is required. The salt crystals are round, while open pan ones were cuboid. This salt will pour from a salt cellar or box and does not need grinding. Different pressures and temperatures produce 'dendritic' where the grains have a spiky surface better for industrial use and snow clearance.

Less people were needed to operate the works and packaging was eventually passed onto other companies. This reduced Winsford's dependence upon salt-making even more.

Only one salt mine survives, expanding under Winsford, Bostock and beyond. It uses huge excavators and trucks to move salt over 130 miles of glistening highway 700 feet below the district. It uses three shafts: a large one at Meadow Bank for bringing salt to the surface, a smaller one for the miners, and one at Bostock for maintenance works. The mine uses the lower bed where flooding is hardly known. It was first opened in 1844 when Herman Falk employed Thomas Phipps to direct the work. He excavated two shafts which can still be seen, though they are now blocked. It was closed in 1892 by the Salt Union because Northwich mines were less costly. It reopened in 1928 after the Adelaide mine was flooded.

In 1940 a new shaft was sunk to the lower bed by the Ministry of Works. The growing need for salt to keep roads free of snow created new markets. The mine produces more salt a year than all the Victorian salt works. It is stockpiled ready for the winter demand. Excavation is in the area between the Industrial Estate and the King Street fault and extends as far north as Davenham. It avoids built-up areas which might be affected by explosives. Only once has there been any risk of subsidence; in 1969 rumours filled the town that the whole place was about to collapse. That was because an old boring through an underground brine flow had not been filled properly, but it was soon brought under control.

In 1992 reorganisation of ICI saw the sale of the salt-making operations to a new Company, which used the old name of Salt Union. It is worth the drive along New Road to see the surface workings and the vast stockpiles which are built up each year. The company aims to excavate enough during the summer months to be ready for any demand in winter. Winsford salt contains a certain amount of sand, so that when it gets wet, the outer surface forms a 'thatch' which is waterproof, and so the salt can be stored without need for cover. As a result there is not a town in the country that does not have a pile of Winsford salt awaiting winter weather.

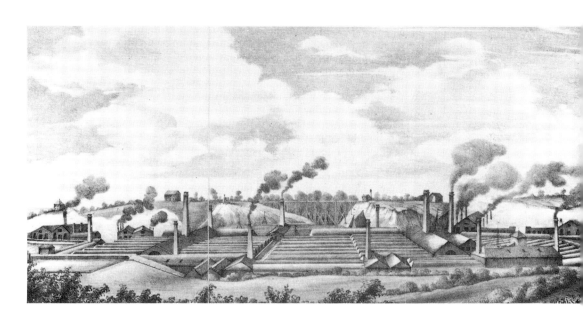

Furnival's Salt Works, Wharton, in 1832 shortly before he became bankrupt. (CM)

ABOVE: Salt works at Meadow Bank – try counting the chimneys! The meander in the foreground has now been filled and the river flows through Verdin's Cut; the site is one of the stockpile areas for the Meadow Bank Mine. (C) BELOW: Labourers making common salt, drained on the floor (hurdle) at the side. (WTC)

ABOVE: Filling tubs and transporting fine salt on a two-wheeled truck,
around 1900. (CM) BELOW: Loading coarse salt into a flatboat on the
Weaver using two-wheeled carts. (C)

ABOVE: New Bridge Salt Works, formerly owned by Verdin's, at the turn of the century. BELOW: Sir William Henry Verdin's home at Highfield became the Victoria Infirmary when he moved to Darnhall Hall. (C)

LEFT: Darnhall Hall, home of Sir William Henry Verdin, one of the 'salt king' family. (C) RIGHT: Moulton's only public clock allowed workmen and factory owners to regulate hours worked. (C) BELOW: Aerial view of the Weaver and its works, early 20th century. (CL)

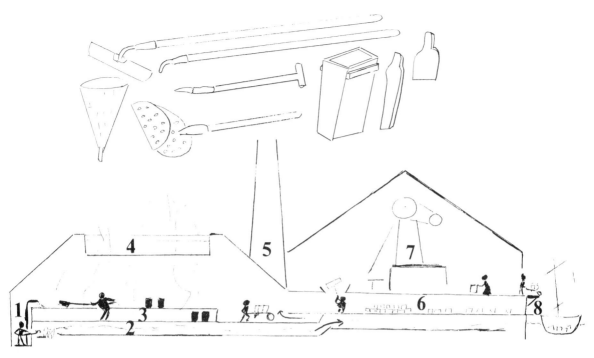

ABOVE: Tools used in salt making: from the left – salt barrow or basket to drain salt, long handled rake, dodging hammer, perforated shovel, lofter's spike, elm tub, mundling stick and happer.
CENTRE: Cross section of a pan house. 1 stoke hole, 2 pan, 3 tubs being filled, 4 open roof to let steam escape, 5 chimney, 6 salt drying in the hot house, 7 crushing mill, 8 loading on the river.
BELOW: More salt works from the air. Notice the Cheshire Lines Railway and New Road. (CL)

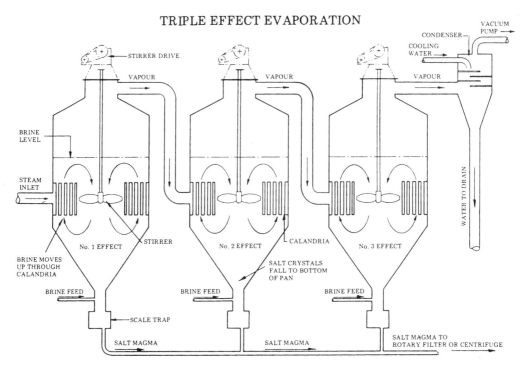

ABOVE: Diagram of the multiple effect salt works first used in Winsford, collecting steam to heat all but the first container. A vacuum is caused by this process in the pan and the works were always known as 'Vacum'. (ICI) BELOW: The Mayor of Over, backed by over 100 police and a similar number of Hussars, threatened to read the Riot Act to the 1892 strikers. They assembled on the steps of the Salt Union Office.

ABOVE: Women stitch bags of salt for export at the turn of the century (CM) and BELOW: they pack salt in 1936.

ABOVE: The name Falk was noted for quality and used in marketing long after the Company was absorbed into the Salt Union. (CM) LEFT: One of the 'bass houses' built by Falk at Meadow Bank (CM) RIGHT: The original Meadow Bank School, built and designed by Falk and constructed from bass. (CM)

Victorian New Town

Victorian Winsford gradually became the leading salt production town in the Kingdom, if not the world. Salt works lined the Weaver at Meadow Bank – making the name singularly inappropriate! Each works had a chimney to each pan so that Winsford probably had more chimneys in half a mile than any other town on earth, burning over 250,000 tons of coal a year. Low grade coal was used to keep down costs. Local school children were sent with a bucket and a poker to search the tips for cinders and bits of unburnt coal to keep the only fire in the house burning. This was used for heating, cooking and provision of hot water, not to mention drying laundry. Cinder picking was particularly common during periods of unemployment and slump and continued up to the 1930s.

The Weaver was Winsford's lifeline and was plied by a special, wide, flat-bottomed sailing barge known as a flat. It had a sail but was pulled by a horse when winds were not favourable. It sailed across the Mersey estuary to unload at the Liverpool docks for export. Much of it went to West Africa through the port of Lagos and 'common Lagos' was the name of a particular grade of salt. Lagos is still a placename in Winsford.

Conditions for the boat people were often less than perfect; sometimes the cabins became wet and far too many people crammed into the boat. Children slept under the canvas covers on the salt or coal. When officials came round they were hidden. Each vessel probably had more people than regulations allowed, and children who should have been at school were not.

The watermen knew Liverpool well, having their favourite drinking places there. If they were lucky, their wives and families could join the men for a journey to Liverpool to buy special items such as a new hat or dress. The men tried to buy a new boatman's cap each year. Sometimes chairs were fitted to the decks, such as for outings for Sunday schools on Frodsham and Overton Hills. A Sunday school outing from the Congregational Church in1904 involved two barges from the Salt Union; one for adults and one for children. They were pulled by the steamer *Pacific*. The Over Silver Band led them in procession to the boats and the day was spent at Dane Bank Farm, where refreshments were provided. It cost £9 11s 6d. Other flats took the townsfolk *en masse* to attend the 1895 elections in Northwich.

Coming to work in the Cheshire salt works was a common means to emigration. Men would work as labourers to save up the fare to the New World and worked their way down the Weaver to Liverpool as deck hands.

Wharton and Winsford were essentially new towns in the 19th century. Wharton's provision of schools, places of worship, a police station, market hall etc was aimed at serving a population which grew from virtually nothing to around 1,400 in 1841 and 1,900 in 1851. The Census only recorded those at home that night, some of them were absent as they were on board vessels. As Wharton was separately administered from Over this caused duplication of services such as school boards, police and markets. A 1777 map shows hardly more than half a dozen houses in Wharton.

Wharton and Over can be compared in White's *Directory* of 1860. Over had fire and life officers, inns and taverns, bakers and flour dealers, beerhouses, blacksmiths, boot and shoe makers, brewer, butchers, chemist and druggists, farmers, joiners and cabinet makers, linen and woollen drapers, milliners and dress makers, salt works, shopkeepers, surgeons, tailors, watchmakers, wheelwrights, wine and spirit merchant, an omnibus and a carrier. There were 33 other names recorded as professional people, ranging from a veterinary surgeon through a saddler, clog maker and cooper to members of the clergy.

Wharton (which included Winsford) also listed 33 professional people, some with water interests, including ship builder, timber merchant and rope spinner. Some had more domestic leanings, including a cutler, a clock and watch maker and a straw bonnet maker. The grouped occupations were beerhouses, inns and taverns, boot and shoe makers, farmers, salt works proprietors, shopkeepers, tailors and a wheelwright. The picture which emerges is of two busy, self-contained and virtually self-sufficient communities with salt as their main industry. There were 33 proprietors named. Their employees did not qualify for entry as White only listed the middle and upper classes.

Only two establishments in Wharton but nine in Over claimed to be inns or taverns but there were nine beerhouses in Wharton with only eight in Over, showing a certain social difference between the drinking classes.

Winsford was not only divided by the river; there were those who drank and those who would not. Winsford had over forty licensed houses but, from the turn of the century, magistrates could take away the licence of houses felt to be surplus to requirements. Today the number is around half that. The Winsford and District Temperance and Band of Hope Union or the Primitive Methodist Prosperity Band of Hope both put on magic lantern shows to demonstrate the evils of drink and the good of sobriety. Church and chapel people would not enter each other's places of worship unless to attend a wedding or funeral, and then reluctantly.

The Queen of Love, a novel of 1894 by S. Baring-Gould, is clearly set in Winsford, which is called 'Saltwich'. The inhabitants either lived at the bottom of the hill which they call 'Heathendom' or in 'Jewery' at the top of the hill. The story comes to a violent conclusion when the ground subsides under a circus attended by most of the population of 'Heathendom'. The 'soiled black cottages' of the lower town were mostly cleared away as pre-war slum clearance or post-war development. They contrast with the bright new houses with gardens at the top of the hill.

While Moulton never became part of Winsford Urban District, it was covered by the Local Board. It grew as another completely new village dependant upon Winsford's salt works. It developed when the New Bridge Salt Works were opened in 1831, with access through a tunnel under the railway line. The cottages were built on the hill-top, slightly north of the works, to avoid the smoke.

The first cottages were built in pairs in the 1830s around Chapel Street and Chapel Lane. The Congregational and Primitive Methodist chapels are little bigger than cottages. The few gravestones in the Congregational chapel-yard almost all show a number of children who died young. Parents seem to have lasted into their '80s. If you survived childhood you could look forward to a ripe old age. At that early stage there was no pub as non-conformists were mainly non-drinkers. The National Schools were opened and in 1871 a cottage with a clock in the front wall was built. It was a law that a public clock had to be available for the workers, who could not afford a clock themselves. Managers had to check their works clocks against it and workers could see if they were on time. Each settlement had its own time regulated by its own clock until the introduction of 'railway time' so that trains could run to a national timetable.

In 1865 the Verdin family, who had made their profits operating boats on the Weaver, purchased the New Bridge Salt Works and adopted Moulton as their own. They presented the new church of 1876 and village institute. In1888 the Verdins joined the Salt Union with other Meadow Bank Companies though, as major shareholders, they continued their involvement with Moulton.

The building of Church Street and Regent Street as an impressive factory colony took place under the Verdins with long rows of tall, terraced houses. Behind each house was a wash-house with its own boiler and a drying ground was provided. The 1891 Census returns reveal much about the make-up of the settlement. The average parent/householder was between 35 and 45. Most had families of several children and most of those were in school. Those who had left school worked in the salt works, and not one married woman had a job. Birthplaces recorded are rarely local, with groups from Manchester, Somerset, Lichfield and other parts of England. The few who did not work in salt-making worked on the railways.

All these children prompted the need for a better school, and the National School was rebuilt in1894 by the Over School Board with funds helped by Sir John Brunner. The schoolmistress was Amelia Offer, aged 29, who lodged at the village store. Her birthplace was Devizes in Wiltshire. The same year gave Moulton its own branch of the Winsford Co-op, and the status of a civil parish separating it from Bostock. In1896 the Red Lion opened, giving the village its second pub.

While Winsford's inns and beer houses provided most of the available leisure facilities, there was a strong teetotal element under the influence of non-conformists. They provided facilities, teetotal societies and events in their Sunday schools as alternatives to drink. Winsford had its branch of the Rechabites, who vowed not only not to drink but to refuse to step into a place where alcohol was served. Victorian irony prompted the naming of one of the pubs on High Street as the Rechabite's Rest.

Apart from the churches and pubs there was a timbered Town Hall in Winsford Market Place, which provided facilities for lectures and dancing. The first silent movies were to be shown there. Amateur musicals and concerts were popular and Winsford even boasted its own band of blackfaced minstrels. There were brass bands from the Volunteers, the Temperance Band, the Salvation Army and numerous choirs, along with the Philharmonic Society. The retired headmaster of the Board School, Mr W. H. Tolfree, was the manager for many years. Local prophets of doom always claimed it was about to fall into the river as the 'stage' end overhung the crumbling river bank, supported on wooden columns.

The Drill Hall was also used for lectures on 'improving' topics. When a lecturer on art produced plaster-casts of classical sculpture, a voice from the back called out 'them statues have got no clothes on'. The lecture continued with the statues draped in towels.

One of the most significant attempts to change the face of Winsford came in 1869, when Abraham Haigh built a massive cotton mill, using natural water springs for its boilers, on Well Street. The streets around were built by him to house workers recruited from cotton towns, especially Bollington. They were given a loan to cover the cost of moving. A new village sprouted up with shops, chapel and pubs.

The mill caught fire in 1874 on the night before it was to be sold. It had been left uninsured for a few hours and Haigh was bankrupted by the disaster. His son lived in poverty as a lodger in a local cottage afterwards. Eight people died in the fire and are buried in a communal grave at St John's.

Harriet Whitehead had her 13-year-old daughter working with her and had taken her three-month-old son to breast feed when needed. Trapped on an upper floor, she realised the only chance to escape was to jump into a tank of water above the boiler. Her daughter managed to do this, but the baby fell short when thrown; it was killed falling on the cobbles. When she tried herself, her dress caught in a window catch and she was left hanging, helpless, in the smoke and flames.

Fire engines from Winnington, Tarporley, and Middlewich attended but Winsford had no fire engine at the time. Ironically one was actually being built on order at Manchester – the *Albert* became the town's pride when it arrived.

The bodies were taken to the Wheatsheaf, where the coroner's inquest was held, before they were buried in a communal grave in St John's churchyard. A second 'Over Mill', for producing fustian, opened in John Street in 1886.

The other main industry in the town was one which gave it a reputation for appalling smells. Meat was processed here into sausages, pies, and other meat products where the origin of the meat could not be detected. Old animals and those which had died in birth, let alone sick or wounded ones, were used without regard. Known as 'slink butchers', the trade had its centre near the bridge and gave Fletcher Moss the subject for the most depressing descriptions of Winsford. 'Up the long hill from Winsford to Over we trundle our bicycles amidst perfumes indescribable…The long filthy hill to Over…could hardly have been worse than it is; the light of the sun is darkened by the smoke, the stench is horrible; what should be fields are tracts of blackened slime where the skeletons of the trees stand gaunt and withered'. This was Winsford at the height of its prosperity!

Not far away the bone works of the Bradbury family ground the bones that were left, to make artificial fertilizers and for bone-meal used in the production of bone china.

One of the most significant steps in its commercial development came in1860, when James Leigh, a cobbler, and his friend William Denson (formerly of Rochdale) agreed to form a Co-operative Society for Winsford. The bellman was sent around to invite people to a meeting in the Navigation Inn. A deputation was sent to the home of Co-operation at Rochdale and an official meeting was called for 22 October 1860.

Capital was raised to buy the land and build a shop at the bottom of Winsford. One man passing asked for whom the shop was being built and, when told. exclaimed 'Who would have thought it?' The committee decided that this was a good name and the foundation plaque was given the inscription 'Who would have thought it? This building was erected by working men for the benefit of the working classes AD 1860'. All the cash was spent on the building and no money was left for stock. So a loan of £250 had to be obtained to start business.

In 1864 there were rumours that the business was in difficulty and this caused a rush of people demanding their cash back. An emergency meeting introduced a six month 'cooling off' clause and the panic was controlled.

The choice of managers was not satisfactory. At the end of the first year only 7s 6d was left to pay a dividend and, when this was revealed at the meeting, the Manager, Joseph Mascal, pulled a knife, injuring one of the committee. The next manager appeared to be so trustworthy that committee members stopped attending the annual general meetings. When he died it was found that the entire records were written on scraps of paper and old bills. It took weeks to sort out and there was even confusion over which property was his and which was the Co-op's. The land for one branch was in his name and many customers believed it was his own store. The Registrar of Friendly Societies was about to issue a summons when two members of the committee travelled to London to explain the situation.

Revivals of old traditions, like that of the Borough of Over, were a common expression of Socialist ideals of returning to the values and traditions of old England. One such was a May Day procession with a crowning ceremony and fête on a field behind the Guildhall. Each school sent its pupils to march in best clothes behind their school banner.

John Henry Cooke remembered the terrible state of the town when he became solicitor to the Local Board of Health in 1875. 'Winsford at that time had no public water supply, or lighting, and the footpaths were not formed or paved. People used to get their water from a public pump opposite the street now called Well Street. There were privvies and cess-pits in abundance. A water closet was unknown. There had been many deaths from cholera in 1866' (and earlier). The Board did their work well and the Winsford Urban District was considered a model authority in the county.

Cooke continued to control town development as Clerk to the Urban District Council, secretary of the School Board and Recorder of the Borough of Over. He prided himself that, during his term of office, 90% of houses had received running water and sewers. The town had its own water purification works and water tower by Oakmere with another tower to keep up pressure in the pipes at Over. The gasworks behind the High Street/Weaver Street junction were opened in1857 by a private company. It is said that the lamp lighter started from Wharton and cycled through the town, hindered by only having one leg. When he reached Delamere Street he proceeded to put them out again as he returned to Wharton, so people carried candle lanterns when out at night. As a result Winsford was known as 'Darktown'. Only the ornamental fountain light standard by the bridge was kept on all night to guide the mail coach.

By the 1890s Winsford was a showplace for sewerage processing. Representatives came from other towns to inspect the filter beds on either side of the Flashes. They used basses from the saltworks as homes for the microbes which cleaned the water. It became known as the 'Winsford Method'. The idea was suggested by the second Lord Delamere. He was not only the first Chairman of the Urban District in 1895, but the first member of the House of Lords to be head of a local authority. Children were less interested in the technicalities but broke down fences to get at the tomatoes which grew in profusion from seeds which had passed through the system.

Civic dignity was added to the Council by Sir William Verdin, who presented a chain of office in 1895, now one of the most impressive chains in the county, with over 100 shields bearing the names of previous holders. He also presented the red, fur-lined robe and black hat for the Chairman, while Sir John Brunner presented the Chairman's chair and desks for the Council Chamber.

Something of the nature of the 19th century is explained by building regulations introduced by Parliament. Pre-1850 buildings are lower and tend to be built in groups of two or four, joined together to form long rows. In the 1870s the only true terraces were built around the Over Mills. From the 1880s the majority of building seems to have been respectable semi-detached houses, often with a date stone and name. Often a row of houses with dates a year apart show where a builder built the first house and then proceeded to build matching houses for customers. This is despite the other evidence that shows decline and poverty at the same time.

The first national involvement with building regulations came in 1848, the year of revolutions on the Continent and of cholera in this country. The Public Health Act laid down basic requirements for housing. From 1864 plans had to be submitted for approval and a further Public Health Act of 1873 gave local authorities more control of housing. The Building Act of 1890 gave them permission to construct subsidised council housing and to demolish unsatisfactory property.

There is evidence that often people 'lived above their means'. Weaver Street was built with small cottages to the north in the first half of the century. When the south side, with views of the Flashes, was developed, it was with large ornate villas. One pair built in Coronation year (1901) even has a portrait of the King between the doors. Each had a bay window with an aspidistra, and a piano could be glimpsed beyond. Rumours started that the people who lived there were too mortgaged to afford good food so they had treacle butties for Sunday dinner. It was nicknamed 'Treacle Can and Piano Row'. Not to be outdone, Wharton had 'Skin Pudding Row', on Station Road. The little early Victorian cottages all have long narrow gardens for self-sufficient vegetable gardening and pigs were kept at the back for bacon, black and white puddings and sausages – hence the name.

In line with all this building, John Henry Cooke was keen to encourage banks and 19th century society encouraged saving to buy and furnish one's home. The Co-operative Society encouraged investment of dividends in shares. The Building Society was established as early as 1840.

ABOVE: Fustian making in one of Winsford's mills. Fustian is a coarse velvety material ideal for work clothes and is made by incorporating special wires in the weaving. These were cut free by women walking the length of the cutting table (C) BELOW: The massive cotton mill built by Abraham Haigh used natural wells in Well Street to make steam for use in the spinning and weaving of cotton fabrics. (WTC)

ABOVE: Spinning mules such as these occupied the upper floors. LEFT: The monument to those who died in the Haigh factory fire with St John's Church in the background. (C) RIGHT: Haigh built Over Hall as his home, but lost it as the insurance had been allowed to lapse for a few hours when the fire broke out. Later it was used as the UDC Offices.

LEFT: Haigh's factory chimney was left standing as a landmark for over 50 years, but RIGHT: down it came on 15 July 1904. BELOW: Assembled townsfolk examine the ruins. The bricks were used to build the houses in Upper Haigh Street.

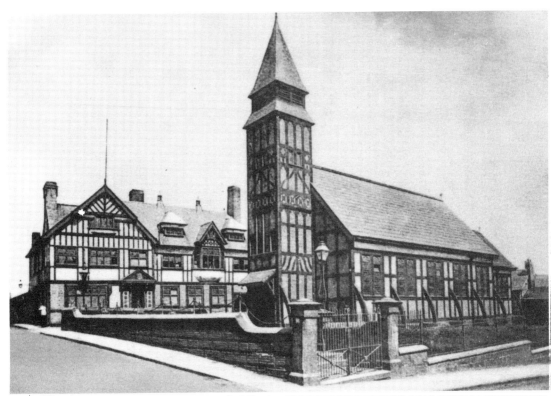

ABOVE: The second Waterman's Church was built in timber-frame to resist subsidence; with the Old Council Offices behind, looking down Church Street. LEFT: Douglas's drawing of how St John's would look. (St J) RIGHT: St Paul's Methodist Chapel between the Wars; with its complex of school and function rooms it was the largest chapel in town.

ABOVE: The 'streaky bacon' Congregational Church designed in Byzantine-style by John Douglas. The old cottage went in the '60s.
BELOW: Whitegate church was remodelled by Douglas.

ABOVE: Wharton Church from a post card posted in 1937. BELOW:
'A bit of old Over'. (MH)

In the Countryside

Winsford, more so than many other towns, is surrounded by attractive estate villages, which developed in the 19th century under enthusiastic patronage from the lords of the manor. Whitegate, Marton, Bostock, Church Minshull and Little Budworth are among the prettiest villages in the county. Rabbits and pigeons from the woods, along with fish and eels from the Weaver formed useful additions to diet, especially in times of unemployment.

Each village has picturesque cottage orné-style housing provided by the Victorian landlord in an olde worlde wooded setting. There were obvious class divisions but life on an estate was felt to be preferable to work in the salt industry. Older children of large families were found jobs cleaning in middle-class houses or helping to maintain the residential part of hotels while still at school. When they left school they were already well-trained with a reference and took up work in local country houses or farms. If they worked well and were respected there they might gain references for more senior posts elsewhere and could rise to become butlers or housekeepers in charge of large staffs.

Each estate was self-supporting and work was provided for the tenants. At Bostock a laundry was operated by women from the village who did the washing from the great house and the estate. A village institute and reading room were provided next to the village green, with a library which became a social club. When the old oak tree, which marked the centre of Cheshire, had to be felled, it was replaced by a sapling from one of its acorns in 1888. The estate carpenter made items of furniture from the wood. Whitegate had a communal bakery behind the post office, where housewives took their own bread to be baked. The cinders were thrown outside, hence the name Cinder Hill.

House parties, where guests spent the weekend bringing their own servants, were common. Houses like Vale Royal added suites of rooms (designed by Blore) to cater for such influxes. Many of the estates and other large houses, such as Over Hall and Crossfield House, had large gardens with several gardeners. There were heated greenhouses for production of grapes and other exotic fruits for the table. Vale Royal had a palm house and orangery, where the trees were nurtured and were taken into the dining room when laden with fruit, so that guests were able to pick dessert straight from the tree. Paternalism was common at big houses. At Over Hall in January 1883 a tent was erected in the grounds, there were fireworks and presents were given to tenants from a tree with 200 candles, marking the engagement of the eldest son.

Even smaller houses employed numerous staff. Early this century, when Mrs Newall lived as a widow at Wharton Hall, she employed six full-time and two part-time maids, and four manservants, including the chauffeur and houseboy.

The landlords encouraged temperance, none more so than Lady Delamere, who ordered the Black Dog and the Rifleman (in the white house facing Whitegate village green) to close in 1870. She did not approve of tenants going for a drink after attending church. When she discovered that they had transferred their trade to the Plough on Beauty Bank, she arranged that it should only be given a six day licence –

a situation which lasted for almost 100 years. It was, perhaps, with an ironic sense of disapproval that the land given for a Methodist (teetotal) chapel in the village was right opposite the Plough.

An unexpected problem was caused by this, as the village boy sent to light the chapel boiler came from a family that would not enter a public house. A Jewish maid at the pub was not allowed to light fires on the Sabbath and waylaid the first person, inevitably the boy, to light them for her. He did not like to refuse but was terrified that his father would find out he had set foot in the pub.

Transgressions against the estates were severely treated. The Vale Royal and Darnhall estate books contain frequent references to taking poachers to the Chester courts. On Christmas Eve 1828 men were seen with guns in the woods around midnight near Darnhall Hall. When spotted, over 20 armed poachers emerged from the wood, frightening the 'keeper, who retreated to the Hall. The men surrounded the Hall, taking potshots at pheasants. They withdrew with the killings for their own Christmas dinners, and plenty of others to sell.

No word was heard for a time until they were traced to Nantwich. Arrested and put on trial before the local JP, a riot ensued when they were taken to the Chester County Court. The poachers were sentenced to transportation, and were already on the prison ship when reprieve arrived. So much ill-feeling was raised by the case that the authorities sought a way out. When a lawyer noted that the court records simply said they were seen at 12 o'clock, this did not specify noon or midnight. The men had been charged with carrying guns after dark, a law intended to protect against rebellions. Insufficient evidence of the correct time had been produced, so the convictions were not valid.

The owner of Darnhall, Squire Corbet was shouted out of the hustings at Nantwich when he stood for election as an MP in 1837. Yet other accounts point to a kindly paternalism. He roasted a bullock for the tenants every Christmas and was once seen to give his overcoat to an old man he spotted shivering after coming out of St Chad's Church. The attractive wooded countryside which survives at Darnhall was mainly due to his planting.

Similar ill-feelings were aroused following the fire at Oulton Park which destroyed the mansion in 1926. Although the house was successfully evacuated, six men died when a heavy, lead water tank fell through the salon roof. They were trying to rescue art treasures and it was felt their lives should not have been risked to save the possessions of the wealthy. At the time it was believed that political extremists had caused the fire deliberately, because four other country houses had been destroyed in only a few months. Investigation disproved this theory, but in the year of the General Strike feelings ran so high that no attempt at rebuilding was ever considered. The house was bombed in the War and in 1954 the estate was leased to build the motor racing circuit. The high wall, built to keep deer in and poachers out, was ideal to stop anyone watching the race without paying.

Bostock Hall was sold to Manchester Corporation as a school for disturbed children when death duties for three members of the family had to be paid in quick succession. The Corbets left Darnhall to live on their Norfolk estate and were succeeded by the Verdins (the salt proprietors). They moved to their Herefordshire castle after selling their local works to the Salt Union.

The third Baron Delamere of Vale Royal was a big game hunter who was responsible for settlement in the White Highlands of Kenya. His memoirs were published as *White Man's Country*. For many years Vale Royal was let to tenants including the millionaire, Mr Robert Dempster. The fourth Baron came back to live there for a short time in 1934 but returned to Kenya, where he was to become involved in the *White Mischief* case, later marrying a chief suspect in the murder of Earl Errol. The county purchased it, intending to develop a police training college. This was abandoned and it became a hostel for Polish workers at ICI, who developed their Salt Division Offices there from 1954 to 1961. After years of abandonment and uncertainty it is currently being restored as a golf club and flats. The landscaped parkland of the three estates survive as some of Cheshire's most picturesque landscape. Each has remained as an estate village virtually unaltered since Victorian times.

Over Hall was also used by the army in the War and Reginald Barton, the leading light on the Urban Council, having established a new home, gave it to the town. The grounds became a park and the walled garden was lawned for the crowning of the carnival queen, with troupe dancing which could only be seen if entrance was paid.

Nearby Crossfield House was the home of John Henry Cooke. He was famous for his gardens and fine orchards. One local rogue was in court accused of stealing apples, which he denied. When the JP commented they were nice apples which looked like Grannie Smith's 'They're not they're John 'Enries' he replied indignantly, but incriminatingly. Large houses went out of fashion and Cooke lost his two sons in the First World War. Big houses were expensive to maintain as servants were difficult and expensive to find in the 20th century. Crossfield House was split to form three dwellings while the stables in the walled garden were converted to a bungalow.

Old farmhouses also fell victim to changes. Knights Grange became a pub when the lands were purchased for building the Grange Estate and recreation grounds. Oak House lost its land to new estates and, after being let to a private tenant, was demolished in 1994. The Nun House farm also went to make way for new housing. In Victorian times High Street and other streets ran through farmland and farms were sited near main roads. There are Victorian engravings of chickens feeding in the road outside the Technical Schools and the threshing machine could be glimpsed from the street as late as the 1950s.

Farm work and working in the game woodlands on the big estates provided a major source of employment. Temporary helpers, including many children, were employed to help with harvesting and picking potatoes. This caused school absentees as children either worked in the fields or looked after younger children while their mothers worked. Irish labourers came to help with the harvest and many returned to the same farm every year. A special building stood in most big farm yards, providing rudimentary wooden beds and a fire for them to spend the night. Despite the local prominence of the dairy industry, grain was also produced and local water mills worked into the present century. Only the opening of the American prairies in the late 19th century made local grain uneconomic. There were half a dozen corn mills within a few miles of the town, using water power.

Mr Tom Bourne left a wonderful description of life at Knight's Grange, which must have been similar to that on most of Winsford's farms. The house was virtually self-supporting. They grew their own wheat, which was ground at Oulton Mill. Bread was baked in a brick oven which had to be heated by putting twigs and wood inside and lighting the fire with straw. The ashes were cleaned out, then bread, followed by pies, was baked. During the winter five pigs were killed so that there were always flitches of bacon and hams hanging in the kitchen. In the winter a heifer was killed and the meat was pickled in salt, saltpetre and brown sugar.

There were two maids, one for the kitchen and one for the living area who 'lived in' as did two of the six workmen. They received dresses for morning and afternoon with aprons and ate the same food as the family, though wages were poor. The house-boys lived in the house for around two years before going on to farm work. They helped with peeling vegetables, collecting eggs and cleaning for a wage of £2 per year. All ate together but the family and workmen had separate tables and the maids waited on them before having their meal. The family had tea but the workmen drank home-brewed ale. What is now the entrance was the general room or house place and to its left was the kitchen and press room where the cheeses were made. Above the kitchen was the cheese room, where they were put to ripen. There was considerable trade in cheese for export though Winsford salt was apparently too sharp for cheesemaking and Middlewich salt was used.

The farm had a stud of shire horses (five mares and a stallion) for working on the farm and breeding, along with 60 milking cows. Each autumn the basket-makers came to harvest the withies growing on the side of the moat. They were one example of several itinerant craftsmen who called regularly.

The Darnhall estate books provide a reminder of the management of the estate for timber. Many of the stately trees, such as those at Marton Beeches, have outlived their harvest date as the estates are no longer managed in the old way. Trees were planted as windbreaks or as coverts for game birds and foxes. In hedges they provided shelter for animals and people using the roads, avoiding hot sun in summer or driving rain in winter. Avenues of trees were planted as at Vale Royal and woods were planted in valleys to provide lighter wood such as willow and alder, which were often coppiced to harvest as rods or withies. Long winding woods along stream valleys are a feature of the local map. They too were planted as coverts for foxes and game birds.

Most of the large houses had pheasantries, shown on old OS maps, where the young birds were hatched and reared ready for the hunting season. Vale Royal pheasants ate rice specially delivered from Liverpool. The Earl of Enniskillen, a friend who entertained the Prince of Wales (later Edward VII) at his home in Cassia, was Master of the Cheshire Hounds, who met regularly at the great houses around Winsford. Assembling to see the hunt and hounds set out was a feature of life. The name 'Cockstool' in Marton is a reminder of a shooting stool which existed in Victorian times.

In February 1840, a sale was held at the Raven Hotel, so named after the Corbet family crest, *corbie* being an old northern word for raven. Among the timber sold were 106 alder trees, used for clog making, at £19. Clog makers cut the soles by hand in the woods, then stacked them to dry. Seventy-five poplars for masts on sailing vessels went for £93 11s 0d. Other lots included 22 oaks, 20 ash, various elm and alders and 16 Scots firs. Similar sales were held each year. Replacements for the trees were planted; 12,200 young oaks and 500 ash saplings were purchased in Chester for £12 1s 0d. Digging them up cost £1 15s 9d and transport for two carts £1 4s 0d. Seven men were paid to plant them at 10s each per week of six days. In 1851 a workman was paid for cutting seven and a half tons of willows at 5s a ton. The willow went to the Northwich basket works of the Gorst family but 11 bundles of twigs were saved for replanting.

Rents for the Darnhall estates were collected at the Raven twice a year, and ranged from £130 for a farm to £1 for John Betley's pauper's cottage. John Barker, the landlord, was paid £3 3s 0d for dinners for 23 tenants, the estate agent and others.

An idea of catering on a grand scale can be derived from the following which is stapled inside the Vale Royal estate book:

'Stock required for consumption:

10 large oxen or 12 small

120 sheep, large ones for the family and smaller for the

parlour

8 bacon pigs

28 porkers

51 pigs to be kept viz.

8 bacon pigs for the current year

8 do for the ensuing year

28 porkers

5 breeding sows

1 boar

The oxen ought never to be killed under 4 years old.

October Brewing 1852:

Ale about 1100 gallons

Beer about 540 do

There was no store in hand when the above was brewed.'

ABOVE: Funeral card and mount: child mortality was an accepted part of life with numerous epidemics and foul air conditions, not to mention doctor's fees which prevented the poor from consulting them. (THAG) LEFT: To give some idea of living conditions, 15 children survived at this High Street house while another half dozen died in infancy. They occasionally took in lodgers too. RIGHT: Three walls cost less than four, so this small Weaver Street cottage was added onto an existing row in 1862. Circular plaques hold retaining rods in position; the rods passed through the house to protect against subsidence. (WTC)

For Their Own Good

Traffic plied the Weaver seven days a week until 1839. Then the religious revival of the Victorian period persuaded the Trustees to close it on Sundays, as the laxity of the previous century gave way to devout church and chapel going.

A meeting of the Weaver Navigation Trustees in 1839 resolved to build three identical churches and three elementary schools in Runcorn, Northwich and Winsford. The Trustees wanted to be sure that, if the men were given time off, they would go to church and not waste the day. It was realised that watermen would not be able to attend church outside their own parish as pews were rented. Those which were not rented were filled with the parish poor. One of the conditions of the Weaver Navigation Act was that profits should go to improvements in the county. Religion and education were among the causes specified.

The original church, by High Street overlooking the bridge, was a handsome stone structure with a tall spire. It was taken down in 1881 after subsidence damage, to be replaced with a timber one. It became Christ Church, a chapel of ease to St Chad's. This was demolished in 1974 after neglect, as the congregation moved away. Its timbers had rotted beyond repair. A stained glass window was moved to St Chad's as a reminder.

The Navigation Schools were built in Weaver Street. Their headmaster, from 1862 until they closed, was William Dunn. He called his school Dunn's Academy, but to pupils from other schools it was always called dunce school! The elementary curriculum meant that children could attend all three schools on successive days without getting behind in their lessons. The Winsford Schools took over the disused Wesleyan chapel and schools opposite the Library for an infants department. That had been the first Methodist chapel in Over and was put up for auction in 1897 as 'A double fronted dwelling-house and the large school-room, known as the Wesleyan schools and school-house situate on the High Street'. Then it was withdrawn, having failed to reach its £310 reserve price. Dunn used his own funds to pay above the withdrawal price. The building, opposite the Library, became part of Breeze's Forge with shops added to the front.

Mr Dunn was a hard working man who had to raise extra money to keep the school open. Sales of work in the Town Hall (to which special trains ran), and numerous concerts by pupils and staff helped to raise money but finance was a continual worry. It was replaced by the Gladstone Street Schools in 1909.

Religious and educational provision developed together during the early Victorian period, the growing town providing many recruits to the wide selection of religious persuasions. A small Anglican chapel was erected near Wharton Bridges, to serve Bostock and Wharton, by J. F. France of Bostock Hall. The Primitive Methodists also had their first meetings in a cottage by the railway bridge. Wharton was part of Davenham Parish, which extended to the Dane Bridge in Northwich. The parish had more people living in Wharton and Leftwich than in the village itself, so chapels-of-ease were provided. Wharton Church was built in 1849 and became a chapel-of-ease to Davenham. The old chapel was abandoned and its materials used to build the new church. Wharton Schools had been completed in 1846, providing infant and elementary levels of education under church supervision. A small school had earlier occupied the site from 1805. The plot had been waste ground belonging to the Barony of Shipbrook and was given by William Harper.

The old church of St Chad was enlarged in 1904 to the north and in 1926 to the south and east as the Town's tribute to the victims of World War I, and as the church adjusted to a new post-war role. John Douglas was the architect. The building is light and airy. Its eastern door is traditionally called the leper door. There is no evidence of lepers being allowed to listen at such doors and the name is a Victorian invention. In fact it led to the old Vicarage, which was just to the east of the church.

The first public clock in Winsford was provided at St Chad's and caused a disaster when in 1753 the works fell through the floor of the tower, killing the Vicar, Rev Edward Moore. Joseph Lees was another vicar who met a sad end; he was murdered in Welsh Lane when returning from Middlewich. There was no lack of humour in church c1801 when it had 'A Crane for a vicar, a Woolfe for the clerk and the curate is always Young'.

For 50 years prior to 1821 Over had suffered from 'absentee vicars', who took the stipend from the parish but lived elsewhere, paying a curate to provide the services. This was a common practice.

Its situation and difficulties of access in winter made local chapels more attractive than St Chad's. Fear of losing people to the chapels worried Anglicans. In 1863 this problem was tackled by the Lord of the Manor, the 2nd Baron Delamere. He erected St John's Church as a memorial to his departed wife. It was the earliest known commission of the great Cheshire architect, John Douglas. A new parish was created from parts of Over and Whitegate parishes. Delamere commissioned Douglas to redesign Whitegate Church in 1875, and he remodelled the Georgian church in a more ecclesiastic gothic style.

Douglas also designed the Congregational Chapel in 1868, in Byzantine style, with layers of contrasting white and red bricks and a roof patterned in two tones of slate. This was lampooned by art historian John Ruskin as 'streaky bacon style'. It replaced a brick stuccoed building erected as Providence Chapel in 1814. The chapel was built in 1868, and the old one was used for the Sunday School which, by the time new schools opened in 1880, had 21 teachers and 280 children. The minister for much of the Victorian period was John Marshall, known as the 'Bishop of Over'. Ironically the difference between Congregationalists and Anglicans was that the former chose their own minister as they had no bishops. He died in 1880 after 60 years' service and a church institute in Woodford Lane was named after him that year.

Much of Winsford's non-conformist worship started with small groups meeting in cottages. Women took a leading part. Elizabeth Kent provided her house in Wharton and shortly afterwards Elizabeth Huxley made hers in Swanlow available for Methodists. Both were widows and their homes were the first regular meeting places in the town. Small chapels such as Clive were built in the first half of the century. There were two in Swanlow Lane, showing that at that date the rural communities were more heavily populated and the town was not the only focus of occupation. Those in the town had become inadequate by the second half of the century when religious fervour was at its height. They were replaced by tall, airy chapels with a large pulpit, an organ and a balcony with pitch pine pews and glowing brass.

The three main branches of Methodism were represented in the town with Wesleyan, Primitive and United chapels in convenient areas. The Primitive Methodists, for example, had chapels in Wharton and Over. Methodist chapels were served by a supervising minister who operated a circuit of several chapels, attending each in turn. Services were taken by local preachers (men trained from the congregation) on those Sundays the minister did not attend. The chapels and churches gave outlets to many clever and gifted people who had to 'stop earning and start learning'. As teachers, preachers, choristers and committee members, they found outlets for their academic abilities. This applied to rural parts of the district such as Clive and Weaver which retain fine examples of small Victorian preaching houses. The best surviving Victorian Methodist preaching house is Bethesda , in Station Road. It was opened in 1894 and built with a timber frame to replace an earlier chapel wrecked by subsidence.

George Slater, of Woodford Hall, wrote his *Chronicles of Lives and Religion in Cheshire* in 1891, an account of the growth and development of Methodism. His memories covered much of the Victorian period and the book includes material from even older people collected in his youth. One early Winsford preacher he records deserves mention, if only that Thomas Atherton (1777-1859) walked an average of 600 miles a year to preach at outlying chapels and cottages.

There was friction between the Methodists and St Chad's in the early part of the last century. Organisation of local matters was centred on the parish from Elizabethan times until the formation of local boards. All inhabitants had to pay church rates for maintaining roads and the poor, as well as the church, which the Methodists resented. George Slater's brother Joseph insisted on attending the vestry meetings, held in the Blue Bell Inn by the church, where it was decided how to spend the money. He was perfectly entitled to do so and have his say, but it caused resentment among Anglicans. This was worsened by his refusal to pay church rates in protest. This caused the expense of taking him to court – held in the Abbey Arms. The Mayor's court had no jurisdiction over such cases. Yet, when compulsory rates were replaced by voluntary offerings in 1868, he sent his contribution.

Methodists are known as non-drinkers, many signed the pledge and joined the 'Band of Hope. Members from St Paul's Band of Hope did not want to be involved in the rejoicings in the town to mark Queen Victoria's Golden Jubilee. They marched in procession to Slater's home at Woodford Hall. The day was spent in drink-free games. The chapels provided a full social life, which avoided the need to go to the pub. 'Tay parties' were a popular way of raising money.

They also provided Sunday Schools. Originally teaching of the three 'Rs' was provided, along with religious instruction. This was before the 1870 Education Act provided day schools. St Paul's church, for example, had a number of class-rooms and a large room for assemblies, including teetotal wedding receptions. There was a large room with a fully equipped stage, for theatrical performances or the inevitable chapel bazaar. The facilities were rented to the Over School Board for temporary use until the Infants School was completed. The Methodists came together as the Winsford Amalgamated Circuit in 1956. Building the new St Andrew's Church was linked to the closure of four old chapels as part of the redevelopment.

Roman Catholics took over a Primitive Methodist meeting hall in Chapel Street when a new chapel was built on the High Street in 1872. Dropping attendance as the century progressed caused its closure and conversion to two dwellings. The poor attendance might be attributed to the lack of work opportunities for migrant labour in the diminishing salt works, and use of machines in agriculture. Catholicism returned to Winsford with a chapel in converted stables on Ways Green, after the influx of Polish refugees created a post-war need. St Joseph's, a completely new contemporary church, was built on Woodford Lane. Its attendant school and club caters for the influx of Catholics who moved to Winsford in the redevelopment era.

The Salvation Army was hard-working in 19th century Winsford. They gathered for hymn singing around the ornamental lamp post by Winsford Bridge, despite cat-calls from customers of local pubs. It was truly a case of taking the word into places devoid of religion. The various pubs around the Market Place were notorious for drunkenness and other social evils. Men from the boats provided good custom for the public houses and the ladies of easy virtue within them. A 'monkey walk' or place for courting couples was a feature of the lower part of High Street each evening. Children loved to be allowed to go into the Salvation Army Citadel in Weaver Street. They sat around a huge pot-bellied stove and joined in community hymn-singing at times when parents wanted them out of the house.

A British School, under the patronage of Lord Delamere, was established in Over in 1858. It was first under St Chad's supervision, but transferred to St John's when the new parish was formed. It was on Delamere Street, using the former Over Market Hall. Lord Delamere bought it and then spent a further £800 converting it to school use with an adjoining master's house.

The Over Board of Education (there was a separate one for Wharton) opened the elementary board schools on High Street in 1876, responding to the 1870 Education Act. They eventually took on responsibility for all local schools. On the first day 43 pupils attended. The numbers continued to grow so that there were over 200 by the end of the year. Over the next few years the teachers had great difficulty keeping control, as many of the children had never attended school before. Extensions were added over the next decade and a separate infants school opened. In 1909 an unusual structure was built into the stream bank at the end of the playground. It contained a woodwork room in the semi-basement and a cookery room, used by other schools as well, on the ground floor.

In 1902 the Local Boards of Education were replaced by committees of the County Council and school provision ceased to be a local affair. Since that date the Cheshire Education Committee has been responsible for Winsford's Schools.

ABOVE: Examples of typical workers' housing at the bottom of Wharton Hill. (WTC) BELOW: A rare view of the back of a house in Winnington Close, off Weaver Street, with the wash house and privy in the outbuilding. (WTC)

ABOVE: With no planning regulations and limited services, houses could be built in any position or combination, as this view from Gravel Hill shows. (CL) BELOW: Winsford houses tend to be built in pairs – old Station Road.

ABOVE: The only house in Winsford – and it's a pub! The Red Lion has the oldest record of any licensed premises in the town and is the only building neither in Wharton nor in Over. The present building is late 19th century, and the fountain lamp post is clearly visible. (C) BELOW: The Forester's Arms was built in 1882 and was one of over 20 pubs closed down in the district. It stood at the lower end of High Street, and its timber frame was designed to help resist subsidence. It closed in 1913. (WTC)

ABOVE: My grandfather's name over the Weaver's Arms shows this photo was taken in the 1890s; it was closed in the '30s and demolished in the '60s. LEFT: The White Swan before it was demolished in 1964. The name Louis Blackburn on the advertisement suggests the cottages next door were built pre-1910. (MB) RIGHT: Timmy the tipsy toad, which vanished just before the White Swan was demolished; he was to have gone to a new home at the new Swan in Wharton. (MB)

ABOVE: The Market place at the turn of the century. (WTC) BELOW: The old Town Hall, later the Strand and Mr Smith's Club, was originally a venue for assemblies and serious entertainment including lectures, and ended its days with a reputation for late night drinking and risqué entertainment. (C)

LEFT: Plate commemorating the Jubilee of Winsford Co-operative Society in 1910. RIGHT: Dickenson opened on Station Road in 1927 as a cycle store, and has developed into a motor dealership on the same site. BELOW: The original Co-op on the right; the road was raised because of subsidence around 1890. It had no upstairs to save cost.

ABOVE: The Victorian Post Office stood on the lower part of High Street. (CL) BELOW: Photographed in 1892, like the rest of this group, as a record in case of salt subsidence for the UDC; small shops on the lower part of High Street (26 and 28). Mullock's drapery store was holding a sale. (WTC)

ABOVE: Agricultural equipment outside 38 High Street is a reminder of the town's rural setting. (WTC) BELOW: Bowness' shop at 37 High Street stands between the entrance to the Blue Ribbon Army Coffee Tabernacle (temperance society), and the stonemason's yard displaying gravestones, right. (WTC)

ABOVE: The corner of High Street and New Road in 1902, a building used for many purposes, including a building society, the War-time Food Office and the Coal Board. (WTC) BELOW: Skin Pudding Row in Station Road, with large gardens for self-sufficient vegetable growing. The name may derive from householder's black and white puddings or from using skimmed milk. (C)

105

ABOVE: Early 19th century cottages in Crook Lane, with a thatched one behind. (CL). BELOW: Dramatic pictures of subsidence are not common in Winsford, but this photo shows the effect of jacking up the timber-framed house while the next door brick cottages have sunk below the new road level. (CL)

'Tis More Blessed to Give

Winsford owed many of its public amenities to Victorian benefactors and the majority were given in the last years of her reign to mark Queen Victoria's 1887 Golden and 1897 Diamond Jubilees. Wealthy industrialists of the time felt that it was right to facilitate public institutions which reflected their morality. They believed that it was better not to give a small wage rise as the workers would only squander it in the pub. Instead they kept the money and donated a worthwhile amenity to the district. Since then social changes have seen responsibilities for such buildings pass more and more to local authority.

The first monument of any significance in the town was an elaborate cast-iron gas lamp standard with a large base which contained drinking fountains. It was set up outside the Red Lion in the Market Place as if it offered an alternative to ale and was given by John D. Cross of Wharton Lodge, a former salt proprietor.

It was agreed that Queen Victoria's Golden Jubilee should be marked locally rather than by way of a collection towards an anonymous national fund. Decisions on what should be erected took some time. The Medical Officer of Health's plea for funds for a good abattoir was not considered, despite the pressing need. Opinions were split between baths, recreation grounds and a library.

The choice was reduced by local gifts. The swimming baths were presented by Sir Joseph and Mr W. H. Verdin near the Market Place on Station Road. They used a part of Cross's Dock Yard opposite the Fire Engine House to add to the distinction of that part of town which included the Town Hall and Market Hall. The timber-framed hall was 34ft wide and extended for 112 feet backwards. It was opened by Viscount Cross, followed by a torchlight procession from Littler to Highfield House (Verdin's home near the Station) where a bonfire and fireworks finished the day.

The baths attracted swimmers from as far away as Crewe and used local brine which had health-promoting qualities, but the building was destroyed by fire in 1917. The adjoining Fire Station met a similar fate and a new one was built on the baths site. They were both timber-framed to resist salt subsidence. The Council then built open-air baths on the bank overlooking the Flashes in 1934. When they opened with a gala, including a brass band, on Wednesday 14 July, Bob Lievers of Hanley broke the British ASA record for the 500 yard freestyle.

The Verdin family started as Liverpool salt shippers with boats on the Weaver. Like many firms they realised the value of owning and operating both boats and pans. They owned works in Northwich and Middlewich and came to Winsford in 1863. In just 26 years they became the most important and wealthy of all salt proprietors. Raised to the baronetcy they were universally known as the Salt Kings.

J. K. Armstrong of Wharton Hall presented the Wharton playing fields and recreation ground as his Golden Jubilee gift. This was on land which had been used as rope walks and given on condition that a proper access road was made. Lord Delamere presented the Over recreation ground, further reducing the choice. On Jubilee day 1897 over 1,600 schoolchildren were presented with a medal and ribbon at the Wharton ground and then marched in procession to the Over Ground where they sang the National Anthem before receiving tea.

A public subscription was agreed to pay for a Free Library. This required the Local Board to hold an election to agree to adopt the Library Act. This would allow them to raise money from the rates to run the future building. 589 people voted in favour and 355 were against. Winsford was one of only 160 towns to provide a public library at that time. It was opened by Mrs W. H. Verdin in the presence of the son of Charles Dickens. Faced with terra cotta with a high flight of steps and a foundation raft to allow for subsidence, Winsford's first public building included an art classroom at the rear. Both functions accorded with the then popular philosophy of 'self help' and were inspired by a Winsford Exhibition of Science and Art held in 1872.

To compensate people for damage caused by salt subsidence, Sir Joseph Verdin set up a trust fund of £28,000 in Salt Union shares in 1889. No sooner done than Sir John Brunner finally got the Brine Pumping Compensation Act through Parliament 1891 after years of trying. This charged a levy on every gallon of brine pumped, the money from which was to be given as grants in compensation. No one could determine which works was responsible for any given damage and so this fund provided an even way of distributing costs, as the big enterprises paid the most.

As the Verdin Trust was redundant (people could not claim from both) permission was given for it to be used for education, among other local causes. Winsford held the first evening classes in art and science in Cheshire, using schools for adult classes. The Verdin Technical Schools opened in 1895 as an early Diamond Jubilee gift. Built before the larger schools in Northwich it served as a pilot, so that its mistakes were rectified and other improvements made when they were built. This handsome terra cotta building is now an adult education centre and part of Mid-Cheshire College. The trust fund is still used to buy prizes and other funding in the Centre.

Sir John Brunner presented the Guildhall next door as his Diamond Jubilee gift to Winsford; this he announced on Jubilee day. It was opened in 1899 in a handsome Jacobean style. Co-founder of the Brunner Mond chemical works at Winnington, he had limited business interests in Winsford but felt it worthy of his support since he was the local MP and Winsford yielded voters for his Liberal cause. In fact Winsford was a problem because John Henry Cooke was leader of the Liberal Unionist party. They did not agree with the Liberal party's policy on home rule for Ireland and broke away. When Brunner asked Cooke to be his agent he flatly refused and said he was voting against him.

It is often claimed that Brunner was against trade unions. In truth his own men only joined a union after he personally pleaded with them to do so, to prevent harassment from Widnes strikers. The Guildhall aimed to provide a teetotal meeting place for unions and friendly societies who might be too intimidated to meet in the works and tempted to drink too much if they used pubs. Brunner was vehemently opposed to alcohol.

William Henry Verdin moved out of Highfield House near Winsford Station to Darnhall Hall and in 1898 gave it to the town to become the Albert Infirmary. A new operating theatre was added in 1910. Before that, and sometimes afterwards, operations were done at home. Children had to be found places to stay, the main table was scrubbed and bleached, and everything that could be washed was washed and preferably boiled. Payment was made in weekly instalments. X-ray rooms and an extension were built between 1935-6 to mark George V's Jubilee. Eventually obsolete, it was closed after the new hospital opened at Leighton in 1971.

When most of these institutions opened there were elaborate festivities and much speech making. The streets were bright with bunting and flags, and processions took guests to the opening ceremony. Magnificent banquets were prepared for them; refreshment, usually a good tea, was provided for the rest of the population.

In 1900, the local Volunteers, known as the 'Buttermilk Soldiers', (buttermilk was more common than 'sweet milk' as a drink for abstaining workmen, since it was cheap) marched up the High Street before going to the Boer War in South Africa. A statue of a soldier commemorates those who died. Growing patriotism saw the Drill Hall (now Cascade Bingo Club) opened by subscription from local people in 1901 for military training.

Mr J. K. Armstrong of Wharton Hall paid to have the old Salt Union laboratory moved to Winsford and re-erected after World War I as a public hall. It was a popular place for dances and other social occasions but was converted to industrial use after World War II.

The Verdins sold their interest in the local salt industry to the Salt Union to move to Weobley Castle in Hereford. The suicide of Roscoe Brunner in 1926 ended the Brunner local interest. National companies with their headquarters and senior management away from the town saw no reason for making gifts. Lord Delamere took up permanent residence in Kenya and pioneered settlement there. The era of the wealthy philanthropist had passed. Nixon is said to have prophesied that a son born to the Cholmondeleys when an eagle was at Vale Royal would see and do great things. This was said to have happened in the 18th century, but a pair of golden eagles were kept even when the family was abroad. Lord Delamere's pioneering work in Kenya was expensive, so the estate was sold off piece by small piece until in 1912 most of Delamere Street and Marton were sold, leaving the house and the rump of the estate. Then they too were sold after the War – and the eagles left Vale Royal.

The last major donation came from Reginald Barton of Over Hall, who had inherited Garnet's salt works. He gave a piece of land to the town football club which became the Barton Stadium. At first facilities were limited and the teams had to change at the North Western Hotel. No football was allowed on Good Friday.

Over Hall was used by the army in the War; they gave just seven days' notice before they took over. Their original choice was Darnhall Hall, but Over was in better condition and Darnhall semi-derelict, so they changed their minds and commandeered Over Hall. The Stables were converted to barracks and the officers used the Hall. The family was settled in another house by the time the war ended so Barton gave Over Hall and gardens to the Council. Plans to convert it into a maternity hospital were stopped in 1948 when the old Council Offices in Russell Street burnt down. It became the Council's Offices. It was demolished and houses were built on the site after Wyvenn House was completed.

ABOVE: The horse trees were an unusual tourist attraction, for legend
said bloodshed would follow if they were felled; they were – shortly
before the Second World War. BELOW: The Guildhall, not long after
it was opened, in Queen Anne style with terra cotta front.

ABOVE: The Library was Winsford's first public building, now
converted to dwellings. (C) BELOW: The opening of the Brunner
Guildhall, Brunner in the centre in a top hat, on his left Mr Hamlett
the Chairman, the Seneschal with the mace and John Henry Cooke in
wig and gown.

ABOVE: Opening the extension to the Infirmary, John Henry Cooke
has abandoned his gown (right) but the women's costumes show what a
grand occasion it was. BELOW: The 'Buttermilk Soldiers' are off to
fight in the Boer War in 1900.

ABOVE: Parades of decorated 'cycles were a feature early this century, here outside St Paul's Church, showing Breeze's well-known tripe shop opposite. (SO) BELOW: Charity begins at home as mother, daughter and baby pose with aproned neighbours and a penny-farthing pram which must have cost several guineas. The building still stands on Station Road. (CL)

ABOVE: The Verdin open air baths in the 1960s; the tower contained the water supply for the showers needed to remove the salt crystals from the skin. BELOW: Winsford Council employees in front of *Albert*, the horsed fire engine of the 1890s; there are only three women.

Days of Depression

Winsford's development reached its apogee in the last decades of the 19th century. The following half century brought the upheavals of war, which affected the community in many ways. There were changes of fashion and of expectations, a different social structure with the growth of the Labour Party, and years of depression. There was less demand for household and estate staff, and the introduction of mechanised farming reduced demand for workers.

Winsford was affected more than most because it was a town relying on one industry. There was a general decline in demand for salt as new products, such as disinfectants in the home and freezers on fishing ships, replaced some of its traditional uses. Historic foreign markets, such as India, which required vast quantities of salt, reduced their demand to virtually none by producing their own at home. The decline of the number of salt works prophesied by Brunner when the Salt Union was formed continued with dire effects in unemployment. ICI reduced its operations to a single automated works and the salt mine.

A housewife in the 1950s, complaining about Hamlett's smoke on her washing, was startled when the owner looked over the wall. 'If there's no smoke there'll be no work' he commented wryly and, by the end of the decade, both works and smoke had gone. Open pan works would never have survived the Clean Air Acts.

Despite fierce loyalty to the area young people had to look elsewhere for work. The death rate for young children decreased and, in common with trends elsewhere, pensions rose as families became smaller. In Victorian times a family of 10-12 was quite common, since several were likely to die. A big family was an investment in breadwinners – until they married and left home. In the 1930s the Council urged that more babies were needed to counter an ageing population.

In 1915 Dr Garstang, Medical Officer of Health, wrote 'It is out of my power to certify the wholesomeness of the milk... ...food inspection is casual'. In 1916 he wrote 'I have the unhappy conviction that there is an exceedingly large trade in cattle of an exceedingly doubtful quality done in this part of the County'. TB was common until the local authority supervised the creation of Accredited TB-free herds throughout the town. Properly conducted slaughter-houses replaced the Over cattle fair, while the appointment of qualified meat inspectors eliminated Winsford's unenviable reputation for processing poor and suspect meat.

Women had worked in the salt industry from mediaeval times, also in sewing and fustian factories from Victorian times. Not to work was the exception for most single and many married working class women. During the two world wars many more were recruited to make up for the men who were away fighting. In World War I, special trains took crowds of Winsford women to work in the ammunition works set up by Brunner Mond in Northwich.

During the Second War the 'square nag', a sort of ferry at the salt works, created much havoc and amusement as the women tried manoeuvring it across the river to work at salt making. Special nursery classes operated in the infants school so that children started at three years old. Each afternoon they had their nap on tiny canvas beds. This left the mother free to work, and continued as late as 1951 to cope with the post-War baby boom.

John Henry Cooke was horrified to find that wives and children of men who had enlisted in World War I had no financial support. He obtained permission for local funds to be used, and later advised the Government on the needs for such support and war pensions. The work he did locally ensured that war pensions were introduced nationally.

'Little John Henry' was appointed Clerk to the Council in 1894 and retired thirty years later. He was Winsford's leading citizen and took an active part in town affairs. He wore the wig and gown of the Recorder of the Borough of Over on important occasions and guided many reforms through the Council chamber. Cooke also found time to compile and publish a complete list of all the books ever written in or about Cheshire, an account of the Diamond Jubilee and the Cheshire Regiment in the Boer War, besides his novel *Ida*.

One of his achievements was a healthier town. Sanitary provision eliminated many fatal diseases. He was happy to report, when he retired, that when he took the job 'cess pits and privvies were everywhere in the town' but '90% of property had running water and sewers' when he left. The Urban Council was also determined to remove slum dwellings. Many tiny, terraced houses in poor condition were inhabited by large families. These took in lodgers, relatives and casual workers, to help to pay the rent. Brick and timber-framed cottages, built before building regulations, were demolished.

Hill Street, at the top of the long stairway behind the retaining wall on Wharton Hill, was due for demolition before World War II. A century before, it was a respectable street and home to several salt tax officers. By the '30s it was considered sub-standard, but the War ensured it took another 30 years before it was demolished as part of a road-widening scheme. The Council was involved in providing new, sanitary, houses and more than 300 were set up between the wars.

In 1918 the Council established an Infant Welfare Centre or Clinic, with the first Health Visitor, based in a spacious house in Weaver Street. Those were the days before the National Health Service when no medical care was free. In 1929 the Council agreed to pay for all pregnant women to have an examination by their own doctor. Previously many had simply not been able to afford it or did not think it worth the cost. This service passed into the hands of the County Council who extended it throughout the county.

There was little new industry, but the Council made a pioneering move in 1936, by working with the Co-operative Wholesale Society to build a bacon factory. Pigs were more numerous, eating dairy by-products along with household scraps. Most farms had both a dairy and pig sty, but only a handful remain today. This was one of the first factories provided by co-operation between a local authority and a local business. A site was found and the planning stages eased by the Council. The facilities were up to date and different from those of earlier years. The factory was away from town, to reduce nuisance from sounds and smells and had its own railway siding.

At the turn of the century, the Winsford Co-operative Society was a major outfit, with specialist departments and buildings which extended from near the bridge for several hundred yards up the High Street. There were a pharmacy, cake shop, grocery, butcher's shop, men's and women's clothing departments, restaurant, coal yard and milk depôt, and a bakery in Weaver Street. Most of the structures were entirely of wood, to resist subsidence, but they were also a terrible fire risk; if one had caught fire it would have spread quickly to the rest. Fire regulations would prevent anything like that today.

There were facilities to pay by instalments and credit purchases could be recorded in the members' book until pay day. Bread and milk tokens could be purchased, and left on the doorstep to pay for deliveries. This saved the delivery staff the risks of carrying change but also ensured that the housewife could still pay for her needs when spent up at the end of the week. There are examples of Winsford tokens in the Salt Museum. The Co-op opened branches throughout the district so there was one near most customers' homes. Orders for heavy goods were delivered to the door in a box once a week. Customers became shareholders and received a dividend once a year. Divi-Day was a time for holidays or buying special items for the home.

There was another special day, unique to Winsford – Good Friday, when every child was given a rubber ball and shops had special displays in the windows. Its origins are unknown and it died out in the 1960s. Yet another was Royal Oak Day, which did not warrant official approval so disgruntled children chanted:

'Twenty Ninth of May
Is Royal Oak Day, We want a holiday.
If we don't get one we'll all run away.
Where shall we run – down Baker's Lane.
Here comes Mr - - - - - - with a big fat cane.'

Baker's Lane takes its name from an 18th century farmer there.

Another tradition which died out in the '50s under the influence of TV was souling, going from house to house singing the traditional song:

'Soul, soul an apple or two.
If you 'aven't got an apple a pear will do.
If you 'aven't got a pear a ha'penny will do.
If you 'aven't got a ha'penny God bless you.
My shoes are very dirty, my clogs are very clean,
I've got a little pocket to put a penny in.
So up with the kettle and down with the pan,
Give me a ha'penny and I'll be gone.'

Over soulers traditionally had black faces and carried a bell to show that they represented the dead of the village. This apparently came to an end during a soap shortage in World War I, when it proved difficult and expensive to get clean!

The first regular 'bus services between Winsford and Northwich started in 1914. The branch lines still carried salt and were much used at holiday times but gave way to 'buses for regular passenger journeys.

Dancing troupes at local carnivals are a North Western tradition and two operated locally. The Moulton Crow dance was one of a series of revivals of old English traditions at the time and was called 'the relic of the cornfields'. The men of the village dressed as black crows who danced around a straw scarecrow, forming mystic signs including stars and pentangles. The farmer 'shot' a crow and the crow and scarecrow were restored to life to dance off the field. This has the elements of an ancient fertility ritual and was choreographed for carnival performance early this century by a dancing master from Winsford. He involved the whole village. The scarecrow had pigeons in its clothing which were released at various points in the dance. They kept one homing pigeon to the end and released it if they had won the dance competiton. People would assemble to help spend the winnings in the Red Lion when it returned. If it did not, they stayed at home.

The other was the Winsford's troupe – huntsmen who wore red coats whose routine was based around a fox hunt. Both underline the essentially rural nature of the town and both ended in the 1950s. Moulton still holds a Crow Fair and children dance a simplified version of the ritual dance.

The Flashes attracted people from all over the North West and North Midlands to enjoy boating and the refreshments provided on the banks and at the Verdin Baths. There was a small industry hiring boats and manufacturing ice cream to sell to visitors by the river and from vans around the town. Bottles of soft drinks and pots of tea were available; many visitors could not afford much more and probably were teetotallers anyway. The Flashes were advertised as the Cheshire Broads. The hire boats ended after a fatal accident was attributed by the coroner to unsafe canoes. In 1916 when nine non-swimmers drowned after taking a leaking boat out onto the Flashes.

New shops and activities arrived between the wars, including a branch of Woolworths, and next door was a roller-skating rink. Winsford had two cinemas: the Magnet on Weaver Street and the Palace, which took over the battlemented Drill Hall on Dingle Lane, and which is now a bingo club.

The industrial depression of the '20s and '30s hit Winsford hard, especially as it was linked to a dramatic drop in the number of salt works. Winsford had no other big industry to provide alternative work for those who had worked in salt-making or on the river. In the '30s the dole queue stretched from the employment exchange, in Weaver Street, right over Winsford Bridge. Men turned up in work clogs and rolled up sleeves prepared to take any sort of job on offer – but there were no jobs.

Early in the century came the means test, when anything considered surplus to requirements had to be sold before benefit was paid. Twin girls were disappointed that they could not attend the Sunday School Anniversary. It was known as 'sitting up' (because they sat in rows on a platform in front of the pulpit) or 'sermons' (because there were two short ones). They had nothing new to wear and it was the day to show off best – preferably new – clothes. Their Sunday school teachers made them matching dresses and their uncle was so impressed he invited them to tea. He was a councillor and one-time Chairman, but out of work. When they arrived, in their matching dresses and over-awed by his status, all sat formally on orange boxes, ate from a tea chest and drank their tea gracefully from jam-jars. Everything from the home had been sold before benefit was claimed.

An Occupational and Social Centre for the unemployed and their families was set up in the 1930s. It provided recreational facilities and women were shown how to prepare low-cost meals. Sewing classes were given and every child attending was given new clothes to be worn on George VI's Coronation Day. The fabric was donated by well-wishers, including local sewing factories, who gave remnants and large off-cuts. The sewing was done by women at the centre.

The Carnival started in 1937 and continued through the War. The salt industry was still big enough to provide candidates for a Salt Queen competition. Mainly they worked in packing and similar light work; there were few opportunities for women to do office work then. After the Second World War there were so few women in the saltworks that it was changed, to become the Clothing Queen, and finally the Industry Queen. Lack of contestants saw its abandonment when there was only one entry.

Several sewing factories flourished following the invention of the sewing machine, and produced uniforms during the Wars. They had replaced the earlier trade in fustian (a cheap pile fabric used for work clothes) at the mills in Well Street, John Street and Rilshaw. The lifting of rationing created a big demand for new clothes.

During the Second World War many evacuees came to Winsford. An ageing population and the tendency for those men not called up to leave town to look for work, provided spaces for billeting. Children arrived from the cities with a label and a small bag containing a change of clothing and other essentials. They assembled in the Armstrong Hall to receive a bar of chocolate and a cup of tea while they were selected by those who had offered spaces. It was not always a pleasant experience for either side. One Liverpool girl walked home. She had been billeted with an old couple who spoke broad Cheshire. She spoke 'Scouse'. They simply could not understand each other.

On a happier note Anne Rogers (*My Fair Lady*) and Johnny Briggs (Mike Baldwin of *Coronation Street*) were among the evacuees and gained early theatrical experience performing in the town. In those days the ICI siren would sound at 11 on the 11th day of the 11th month. Traffic and pedestrians stopped in the streets and the town fell silent, to mark the Armistice.

There were changes everywhere created by war. Americans were based at Oulton Park and on Wharton Hill. Children followed them calling 'got any gum chum' in hope of getting a rare treat in the days of rationing. Several women left the town as GI brides. The Budworth common land was cleared for exercises; all the trees there have grown since the War. The Oulton deer were slaughtered for meat. Over Hall was an army camp and there were Italian prisoners-of-war in a camp by the Red Lion. The Mundesley Sanatorium was evacuated to Vale Royal. One of those who died at the Sanatorium was the son of Sir David Muirhead Bone, the greatest print maker of the century. He and Lady Bone, the writer, decided to be buried at Whitegate with their son. Later it was used as a hostel for Polish refugees working for ICI.

Schools were supplied with underground air raid shelters and every child had a gas mask. Marton Camp was specially built by Liverpool Corporation to house evacuee children who could not find homes with families in the countryside. Bombs fell on Wharton and Budworth. They were jettisoned from planes returning home from bombing raids on Merseyside, to reduce weight and risk of explosion when landing.

The Crown Jewels are rumoured to have been hidden in the salt mine for the duration of the War. Many official papers were certainly stored there. Other places claim the same distinction but the truth is still a state secret. Many supplies, including raw rubber, cotton and silk, were stored in safety there and a sprinkler system was installed in case of fire. These attracted a colony of black mice who made nuisances of themselves nibbling the tallow candles used by the miners.

After the War many Polish refugees, who has been housed in local camps, were unable to return home and took local jobs in the improved economy of the time.

119

Some with high academic qualifications took labouring jobs with ICI because of language difficulties. In the 1950s almost every edition of the local papers had a story about 'a Pole'. Even today many Polish names are found locally, descendants of these refugees and of those imported by Falk over 100 years ago.

The steel works of Henry Smith came to Winsford in 1946. Involved in building the Mulberry Harbours for the D-Day landings, Smiths used 'the year of reconstruction' to relocate.

The town had hardly managed to get back to normal after the War when, in January 1946 a great flood broke the banks of the Weaver. It had been a long rainy winter and a particularly heavy band of rain moved over Cheshire. The ground was soaked and could hold no more. This heavy flow of water met with an unusually high tide flowing from the Mersey down the Weaver. The water backed up the Dane but was met there by high water caused by the rain falling on the East Cheshire hills. The whole valley from Winsford Flashes to the Mersey was flooded. Boats were rowed around the shops into High Street and Weaver Street and a temporary bridge was erected above the Flashes.

Winsford had barely cleaned up after that when the invalid George VI and Queen Elizabeth included the town in their tour of Cheshire in 1946. Every school was allocated a place, and schools came from as far away as Tarporley. The road was lined all the way from Moulton to Winsford Station and beyond. No official celebrations had been held to mark the end of the War and so it was decided to make this a day to remember. After the King passed by (he did not stop) there was ice cream for every child, followed by circus performances on the Dock Yard and a special tea.

The first family of 11 people moved into the Dene Estate the same week. Winsford was to gain praise as the leading town of its size building council houses after the War.

The post-war Labour Government created secondary modern and primary schools from the old elementary schools and the Albert Infirmary passed to the National Health Service. For the first time people had free access to doctors without the worry of how to pay.

1948 brought disaster again on 17 April just after midnight. A soldier returning home found he was on a train which did not stop at Winsford. Daringly, he pulled the communication cord and jumped off near Wharton Church. Unfortunately an express train, the *City of Nottingham*, was following on the same line and ploughed into the stationary one, causing 24 fatalities and serious injuries to many. Local homes were opened for the stranded and householders were eventually compensated for the rare rations of tea and butter they shared with them. Contemporary accounts do not exonerate the soldier but stress that the accident might have been averted, if the elderly signalman had not been too preoccupied with cooking a meal, and the elderly guard had not delayed, then fallen, when setting the alarm signals for the stationary train.

A second fatal accident near Winsford occurred on Boxing Day 1962, caused by frozen points at Crewe and a temporary fault on the phones. The mid-day *Scot* was held up and could not use the phones. The driver took a chance that it was the signal that was frozen and ploughed into a stationary passenger train, killing 18. Engine No 326 from the passenger train was unharmed and gained notoriety when a few months later it was pulling the carriages of the infamous Great Train Robbery.

In 1949 the arrival of MV *Houndsrug*, a Danish vessel and the first ocean-going ship to reach Winsford, was hailed as a major step in making the town an inland port. Despite a few large vessels also going to the Colin Stewart works for minerals, the silting of the Weaver soon prevented any hope of this. At the time it was hoped to expand Winsford to three times its size as the port developed. In 1953 the town was a mass of red, white and blue and street parties marked the Coronation. Many homes had their first TV for the event and neighbours crowded into those houses which could afford one to watch the ceremony. A new Elizabethan age had begun and within a decade the redevelopment of the town would also begin.

Co-op buildings and the Conservative Club (with many steps) flooded in 1946.

ABOVE: Architect's drawing of the Bacon Factory opened in 1936 and one of the first examples of co-operation between an employer and a council to provide employment in an area needing new work. BELOW: 'The Bottom of Winsford' in the '50s. 'Bus shelters have arrived but the 'seven sisters' chimneys of Hamlett's works still survive.

Bigger but Better

The development of Winsford since the 1950s has been enormous with a 95% growth in population during the '60s alone! The new era of change was heralded by the introduction of self-service shopping by the Co-ops in 1960.

Employment was difficult to find because of the decline of the salt industry and people were forced to look out of town for jobs. Young people in particular left and it seemed almost as if the town was to decline, apart from the flourishing sewing factories employing mainly women. The population was static at about 13,000 as new births barely kept up with the young exodus.

In 1962 the Urban District got together with Manchester Corporation, who were looking to provide housing for overspill populations in existing centres. The experience of building Wythenshawe as the country's biggest estate had raised problems of work, entertainment, shopping and other facilities. Adding new estates to Cheshire towns like Winsford seemed an ideal answer, since shopping, leisure and educational facilities were already in place.

The first such estate was the Grange, started in 1962, and the Industrial Estate opened the following year. Advertising at the time stressed the rural pleasures of Winsford as 'the town in the country'. It suggested a range of houses from those at a weekly rent of £1 1s 6d for a family of six with a weekly income of £12 per week to others at a rent of £1 9s 6d for a family of four earning £16 per week. New, private, detached houses averaged £2,000 and 100% mortgages were available from the Council. There was an inevitable culture clash between the city ways of the newcomers and the old village ways of the locals.

Before the Grange was completed, let alone fully tenanted, the Corporation withdrew. Liverpool Corporation were only too pleased to take over the scheme and Winsford's local reputation as 'the second Scouseland' was born. The tenants who had moved from terraced houses to live on the estate, which at that time just had opened with lawns and not gardens, named it after the ranch in the popular TV programme – The Ponderosa. Later estates, Mount Pleasant, Glebe Green and St John's, were named to suggest rural comfort. The first was named after a large house which was demolished, the second was built on glebe land purchased from St Chad's. Some were built using experimental methods with flat roofs and white plastic cladding. New residents referred to them as rabbit hutches. The flat roofs were ideal for hot countries where the sun dried the rain, but in Winsford wet roofs soon started to leak.

During the following years the south side of High Street was demolished and replaced by grassy slopes to a new dual carriageway in the valley behind the old street. The north side was retained as a side street with parking. The old town centre was completely demolished and a new bridge introduced to improve traffic flow. A small wood between the two bridges marks the old town centre – 'the bottom [valley] of Winsford'. Few people live in the original settlement of Winsford, which now retains little more than four pubs and a café.

One loss was Mr Smith's Club, (formerly the Strand, and the second Market Hall). It gave its customers 'a meal' as they entered so that it could claim a supper licence, and was notorious for late-night drinking and risqué entertainment. It attracted patrons from all over the county and beyond. Most often recalled is 'Jasper Buckley's' tuck shop opposite the school, one of the last buildings in the High Street and known for selling single cigarettes to children who could not afford a complete packet. One feature was a large built-in chest which had been used for flour when it was a bakery. This was always covered with under-age smokers out of sight of the teachers. Ike Robinson, the oldest barber in Britain, (who charged 4d a time), is also remembered.

The pedestrian shopping centre was built in two stages. Winsford Market moved from a site behind the old Post Office, and new library, post office, health centre, pensioner's centre, leisure centre, Civic Hall and car parks completed the new Winsford Centre. It was built with black brick to blend with smoke blackened cottages, mostly gone before it was completed.

A fountain was designed as a centre-piece, but it managed to splash everyone who went near, and was replaced by the war memorials, removed from the High Street where they were getting damaged. The name Fountain Court remains.

Children were a major consideration in the redevelopment. Most of the incoming population comprised young families so that Winsford could claim the second highest birth-rate and the second youngest population – exceeded only by Milton Keynes. High Street and Wharton Secondary Modern Schools merged at the start of the decade. This had been planned before the war, when segregated education was the fashion. A new school was opened on land purchased off Grange Lane, intended as a girls only school. Changes in County policy saw the Grammar and Secondary Modern merge. The Verdin was, at the time, the biggest comprehensive in the country, until Woodford Lodge was completed, to take half its pupils. Plans for separate sex schools were abandoned and both became co-educational.

Like the Library, both schools were designed for a much larger population than was ever achieved and both have been reduced by half. The Verdin moved entirely into the Grange building and the High Street buildings are used for adult education and small business units. Half of Woodford Lodge is a professional centre, providing courses for teachers from all over the county. Half a dozen new primary schools were provided, ensuring that every child lived within walking distance of a school able to offer a place.

This preponderance of young families provided no great demand for public houses, for parents stayed in with their children. Only one new one (the Salt Cellar) was built, though the White Lion was rebuilt and the White Swan (known as T'Mucky Duck) moved from High Street to Wharton. A large toad lived in the cellar but it vanished after posing for photographs. Knight's Grange was converted to a pub, serving as a clubhouse for the golf course. The Bull's Head and Rechabite's Rest were demolished when High Street was widened. The Bull's Head had the first colour TV in a town pub. It gained national attention when its landlord was allowed to admit Open University students, who could not afford expensive TVs, to watch their programme early in the morning.

Opening a pub in Victorian times was almost as easy as opening a salt works (there were over 40 at the turn of the century) and many tiny converted cottages struggled to make a profit. In the 20th century, licensing magistrates could take away the licence from establishments felt to be surplus to requirements. Numbers have now almost halved though the population is about three times the size.

A similar picture emerges with places of worship. Over 20 existed around the town in Victorian times but five of these have closed and only St Andrew's and St Joseph's have been built during the town's redevelopment.

The Civic Hall was designed for a bigger population than ever materialised and opened in 1967. It was planned to hold 1,000 dancers and be bigger than the Memorial Hall at Northwich, which often had to turn customers away because it was full. The first performers were the Kinks (then topping the charts) but the days of chart-topping bands visiting small destinations were numbered. The hall still provides a variety of local entertainment and is a venue for regional events which few other halls can accommodate.

One of Winsford's best known landmarks arrived by road the same year. The Brighton Belle coaches were taken out of service by British Railways as they were the oldest carriages in use. The Mona Pullman carriage, made in 1933, was delivered to Winsford. It had worked the London/Brighton line and even carried the Queen in 1948. A specially laid track became its home and it is one of the most unusual restaurants in the region.

By the middle of the '70s it became clear that plans were not being fulfilled. Winsford had agreed to take 70,000 new people by 1986. There were promises of new facilities, including hotels by the Flashes, and a riverside walk with shopping and leisure facilities. In 1970 Liverpool Corporation declared that it did not want to send any significant number of new families to Winsford. It was time to review matters. Without the assured population from Liverpool, grants and Government help for more projects would be jeopardised.

The policy had been to provide estates to the west of the town, with an industrial estate forming its eastern limits. This separation of industry and residences was Government policy. 'Buses were intended to take people to work but were never felt to provide an adequate service. In any case demand fell as the age of the car-owning worker arrived.

The major problem for many years was the single 19th century bridge, approached from two directions on both sides. Until the second bridge and a new traffic flow were opened the town came to a virtual stand-still every morning and evening, as hundreds of cars converged on the crossing. Estates built in the '50s and '60s had inadequate parking, which has subsequently been improved.

Winsford had Development Area status which provided grants and other help to industry moving to the town and financial help for overspill residents to move and furnish their new homes. It never achieved the New Town status of Warrington and Runcorn with overall planning. Development was more piecemeal as money was obtained for each new step.

Then Winsford lost its Development Area status and was absorbed into the Vale Royal District Council in 1974. Some of the earlier factories closed because of changes in industry, loss of Government aid and other problems. International Computers Ltd and Metal Box were the largest. ICL relocated when the most modern factory in the town became obsolete and the Metal Box factory closed because it could not adapt.

Winsford became an unemployment blackspot. The Council was left with two large factories which had only been rented and, as the world slumped into depression, new tenants were hard to find.

This change of status created problems. New inhabitants no longer received financial help to move from cities. There had always been some who went back – people who missed the facilities and could not settle in the country. Now even more went back, leaving empty houses on some of the estates, and there was no temptation to encourage new tenants. It was the policy only to offer houses in Winsford to anyone in urgent need of a home from within Royal Vale. This resulted in groupings of people with problems. Today this policy has been abandoned.

Problems arose from the very buildings themselves, which had been built using experimental materials, subsidised by the Government. Some appeared to be a fire risk, while a gale blew the roofs off three rows of houses on the Mount Pleasant estate. From the 1980s there has been a determined policy to improve all the estates in Winsford, never more noticeable than at Mount Pleasant – renamed the Over Estate. The white facades, intended to make them resemble the White Cliffs of Dover! – were replaced by brick facing and interiors entirely refurbished. Walls for the gardens and brick cladding for the houses, along with car parking spaces, have upgraded the quality of these homes.

The Winsford Co-op merged with the Birkenhead Society, building a huge department store in the Shopping Centre, but it failed to make sufficient profit and closed. Other stores such as Woolworths and Tesco also closed down. The depression had returned.

Winsford's problems in the '60s and '70s have mainly been solved. They were not unique to Winsford and are mild compared to experiences in other developing towns, as well as being typical of the age. However, the way that those problems have been tackled has shown the way for others.

Building still continues on all sides of Winsford. It is one of the few Cheshire towns not restricted by the green belts which prevent the spread of the three big cities. The houses built today are larger houses for the private sector, providing for new standards of living. The position of Winsford with its close proximity to the M6 and other trunk roads makes it popular for those commuting to Manchester or other work out of town.

Now Winsford is developing into an attractive residential town with its industrial estates unobtrusively placed on the edge. It is ideally situated for commuters and shoppers, with four cities and a dozen large shopping centres within a twenty mile radius.

The recent establishment of the Vale Royal Offices and County Fire Brigade in the town shows faith in its future. The new Wharton Park development shows the way to 21st century shopping – out of town with plenty of car parking space and a wide selection of goods under one roof. The completion of the new Davenham by-pass provides the town with a direct link to the motorway system.

Futuristic development includes facilities for testing computers in the constant atmosphere of the salt mine and a radio telescope dish operated from Jodrell Bank at Darnhall tracking the stars. Winsford is poised for millennium.

ABOVE: Deirden Street is decorated for the Coronation of 1953.
BELOW: Apart from the decorations for the Coronation, Dene Street is
little changed today. (C)

ABOVE: Shops in the High Street in the 1960s; the Civic Hall occupies this space today. (C) BELOW: Making main frame computers in 1970 at ICL Winsford. The invention of the microchip made the town's biggest employer redundant almost overnight.

ABOVE: First phase of expansion, The Grange Estate, with the older square plots of the mediaeval Borough to the right. Taken from above the Gate Inn, an ancient name which refers to a highway, not a gate. (NAG) BELOW: Mount Pleasant, as built looking over Woodford Lodge. Government policy dictated the plastic cladding and flat metal roofs, neither of which were suited to the Cheshire climate. They were known as 'The White Cliffs of Over'. (NAG)

Council houses on each side and private houses in the centre show the differences in housing provision. Over Hall in its Edwardian gardens is to the top of the photo. (NAG)

The town that never was: 1960s architects' drawings of how Winsford
would look in 1986.

Bibliography

Anon *Hugh Starkey and the Church of St Chad*, 1983; *The Meadow Bank Mine*, ICI, undated

Axon, W.E.A. *Cheshire Gleanings*, Axon, 1884

Beamount, William *Doomsday Book of Lancashire and Cheshire*, Minshull and Hughes, 1893

Barker, T.C. *Lancashire Coal and Cheshire Salt and the Rise of Liverpool*, Lancs and Cheshire Historic Soc, 1951

Bolger, Paul *The Cheshire Lines Committee*, The Cheshire Limes Committee, Heyday, 1984

Bourne, Thomas *Looking Back 100 Years (Knights Grange)* typescript

Brownhill, John *The Ledger Book of Vale Royal Abbey* Record Soc of Lancs & Ches, 1914

Calvert, A.G. *Salt in Cheshire*, 1915

Chaloner, W.H. *Salt in Cheshire 1680-1870* Lancs and Cheshire Antiquarian Soc, 1949

Cooke, John Henry *Ida, or the Mystery of the Nun's Grave at Vale Royal Abbey*, 1912
    The Queen's Diamond Jubilee in Cheshire, Mackie, 1899
    Biblithecia Cestrensis, Mackie, 1904

Cheshire Community Council *A History of Cheshire* (several volumes)
    Women's Institute *Cheshire Village Memories*, 1952; *Cheshire Village Books*, 1994

Cogger, David *The Verdin School Winsford*, Verdin School, 1995

Crump, W.B. *Saltways to the Cheshire Wiches*, Lancs and Cheshire Antiquarian Society, 1939

Crosby, Alan *A History of Cheshire*, Phillimore, 1996

Curzon, Bob *Winsford and Wharton in Times Past*, Countryside, 1986
    J., Brian *A very Royal Heritage*, Silver Jubilee Handbook, 1977

Dodgeson, J. McNeil *The Placenames of Cheshire*, Cambridge University, 1975

Griffiths, C.J.C. *Methodism in Winsford*, typescript, 1986

Head, Sir George *A tour through the Manufactureing Districts of England*, 1835

Hewitt, H.J. *The Building of the Railways of Cheshire*, Moreton, 1975

Hughes, H.J. *Cheshire and its Welsh border*, Dobson, 1966

Irvine, A.S. *The Story of Salt*, ICI, 1872

Kelly *Directory of Cheshire*, 1906

Leigh, Egerton *Cheshire Ballads and Legends*

Lightfoot, T.S. *The Weaver Watermen*, Cheshire Libraries, undated

Lucas, Hedley *Homage to Cheshire*, Independent Press, 1939

Marlow, Joyce *Dingle Days, Memories from Winsford*, 1990, DAN

Morant, Roland *Cheshire Churches*, Countrywise, 1989

Moss, Fletcher *Pilgrimages in Cheshire and Shropshire*, Moreton, 1901

Murrell, A.M. *John Henry Cooke*, Nicholas, 1963

Newell, C.E. *The Brine Pumping (Compensation for Subsidence) Bill*, 1891

Nulty, Geoffrey *Guardian Country*, Cheshire County Newspapers, 1978
    Geoffrey and Sylvester, Dorothy *The Historical Atlas of Cheshire*, Cheshire Community Council, 1958

Ormerod, George *The History of Cheshire*, Helsby Edn 1880

Powell, Francis E. *The Story of a Cheshire Parish*, 1897

Paget Thomlinson, Edward *Mersey and Weaver Flats*, Wilson, undated

Pevsner, Nikolaus *Buildings of England – Cheshire*, Penguin, 1974

Piggot, J. *Directory of Cheshire*, 1828

Price, W.R. *Central Methodist Sunday school anniversary souvenir*, 1945

Richard, Raymond *Old Cheshire Churches*, Moreton, 1947

Rochester, Mary *Salt in Cheshire*, (teachers' packs), Cheshire Museums
    and others, Brochures on the *Salt Industry*, Cheshire Museums

Salt Museum *A Brief History of Cheshire Salt*, Cheshire CC, undated

Samuel, Raphael (Ed) *Miners, Quarrymen and Salt Workers*, Routledge, Kegan and Paul, 1977

Shakland Cox & Associates *Expansion of Winsford*, 1967

Slater, George *Chronicles of Lives and Religion in Cheshire*, Crombie, 1891

Smith, William and Webb W. *The Vale Royal of England*, Daniel King, 1656

Tibbets, Kenneth *Bethesda Methodist Church*, 1965

Thomas, Margaret *Winsford in old Picture Postcards*, European Library, 1986

Thompson, F.H. *Excavations at Vale Royal*, Antiquaries Journal, 1962

Vale Royal BC *An Industrial History in the Heart of Cheshire*, undated
    Vale Royal Guide, various editions; Estate *Sale Catalogue* 1912

Victoria County History, Cheshire Vols 1,2,3

White, Francies *Directory of Cheshire*, 1860

Williams, T.S. *The River Weaver in the 18th century*, Cheetham Society, 1951

Winsford Industrial Co-operative Society, *Souvenir of the opening of the new Central Premises 1901*,
    Co-op printers
    Community Play: *Salt of the Earth*, 1991
    Town Council *Winsford Guide*, various editions; *Coronation Handbook*, 1936; *Winsford* (overspill brochure),
    undated; *Liveing in Winsford* undated

Journals:
*Cheshire Local History Newsletter, Cheshire History, Cheshire Archaeological Bulletin, Winsford Chronicle Winsford
    Guardian, Winaford Record*

Index

All figures in *italics* refer to illustrations.

Subscribers

Presentation Copies

1 Winsford Town Council
2 Vale Royal Borough Council
3 Cheshire County Council
4 Winsford Library
5 Northwich Chronicle
6 Dialysis Unit, Wilmington Hospital
7 Nicholas Wilson

8 Brian Curzon
9 Clive & Carolyn Birch
10 Elizabeth Pardo
11
12 } Stanley Orme
13 Mrs C.A. Shepherd
14 N.J.W. Wilson
15 Alan Woodray
16 Colin Walsh
17 Peter Maddock
18 A.J. Bostock
19 Gilbert Atherton Emery
20 Mr & Mrs E. Goulding
21 Mrs F. Burton
22 Mrs J.M. Mountfield
23 } St Chad's CE Primary
24   School
25 Robert Latham
26 Alan Latham
27 Brian Gaffney
28 Trevor R. Sayle
29 R.M. Harding
30
31 } Alan Buckley
32 Veronica Lewis
33 Mark Shaw
34 Colin Robert Mather
35 Mrs P.L Kosogorin
36 Nich Hughes
37 Nigel Graeme Cope
38 Nicola M. Humphreys
39 Peter Moors
40 Olive Martin
41 Mr K.W. & Mrs J.I.
     Starnes
42 Mrs P.M. Parsons
43 Mrs L.M. Atkinson
44 J.R. Sprotston
45 G. Walker
46 Geoffrey Green
47 Mr & Mrs G.F. Tobin
48 Mrs S. Matthews
49 Alan D. Newall
50 Joseph Anthony Byrne

51 J.T. Brittleton
52 P. Moors
53 Alastair Goodlad
54 Mrs J. Challinor
55 Margaret A. Blears
56 John McCabe
57 C. Games
58 Mrs M.Lumb
59 Marjorie A. Blears
60 Mrs J. Rimmer
61 Peter Royle
62 A.W. Holland
63 D. Ashmore
64 H. Hatton
65 J.N. Astbury
66 J.A. Kitchen
67 A.W. Kennerley
68 Eric Heatley
69 R. Jolly
70 Gladys Cotterill
71 Mrs A. Hardman
72 H. Nellist
73 Andre R. Faux
74 Mrs Elaine Daniells
75 Mrs J.N. Astles
76
77 } Mrs E. Dobson
78 Mrs J. Little
79 Mrs Beryl Hadfield
80 Norman G. Newall
81 Mrs M. Howley
82 L. Jones
83 Ann Lamb
84 Roger A. Owen
85 J. McKay
86 Mary & John Hodgkinson
87 D.&L. Dutton
88 Stuart Redhead
89
92 } Cheshire Libraries
93 K.E. Bentley
94 Woodford Lodge High
     School
95 Grace Gibson

96 Eileen Bowerman
97 Martin & Shirley Soar
98 C. Hickson
99 Michael Weadock
100 F.J. Doyle
101 Terry Dodd
102 A.B. Reade CEng MCE
103 Jenny Tyson
104 Jack Edwards
105 Diane Johnson
106 John Kirk
107 R.W. Deakin
108 George Williams
109 Family History Society
110 Lyn McCulloch
111 R. Lambert
112 H. Buckley
113 John Platt OBE DL
114 St Nicholas RC High
     School
115
116 } J.K. Cross
117 June Sloan
118 Mrs C. Rice
119 W. Bennion
120 John Hatton
121 Mrs Mavis Simpson
122 M.J. Brandon
123 Mrs E. Newall
124 Mrs J.V.C. Bettelley
125 Keith Sadler
126 Roland Ayliffe
127 Andrew Davies
128
132 } Winsford Library
133 Mrs T. Done
134 Karen Eaton
135 Mrs D. Harrison
136 Christine Noden
137 William Stedman
138 B. Jones
139 E.W. Whitney
140 A. Montgomery
141 Colin S. Hoole

142 Rosamund Minns
143 George Sankey
144 Gillian A. Sankey
145 Gavin Kettle
146 Eric Stock
147 A. Leese
148 Brian Dale
149 Mrs M. Bromidge
150 Daniel Richardson
151 Sidney Hatton
152 S. Gillett
153 Graham Norcross
154 Heather Cunliffe
155- Cheshire Record
162   Office
163 Terence A. Judge BEM
164 Dave Ryan
165 Lynn Evans
166 Barbara & Colin Sandbach
167 Maureen Duncalf
168 Noreen Patterson
169 Anthony Hugh McFeat
170 R.D. Garner
171 Ken & Lillian Hartley
172 Donald Runciman
173 J. Hughes
174 Cllr N.R. Harris
175 T.J. Duffy
176
177 - Mrs S. Orme
178 Christine Kirkham
179 B.A. Meager
180 I.M. Shaw
181 Mrs L. Evans
182 Mr R. Blackburn
183 R. Mills
184 Miss M. Cannon
185 Pat Flood
186 Miss Gladys Egerton
187 Mrs E. Bradburn
188 Mrs M.W. Watson
189 B.A. Meager
190 D.A. Hindley
191 Elizabeth Jordan née
    Brittleton
192 G. Snape
193 Mrs J.M. Dunning
194 M.J. Leigh
195
196 - Greenfields CP School
197 A.R. Littler
198 The Robbins Family
199 S.C. Pinnington
200 Margeret Beswick
201 B. Hulse
202 P. Bradshaw
203 Mrs J. Wakling
204 John Bradshaw
205 Mrs Ode
206 Mrs Jo Rourke
207 Mr & Mrs C.D. & B.E.

Prior
208 Mrs E. Stanway
209 Mrs E.J. Williams
210 Mrs Doris Hamlett Bushby
211 Mrs C. Abbiss
212 Hildegard Carden
213 Raymond King
214 Kevin Smith
215 Darnhill CP School
216 George Majewkz
217 Mrs C. Torlop
218 Ralph Mills
219
220 - Mrs Sylvia Needham
221 Kevin Wilde
222 J.M. Ryan
223 G.D. Hindley
224 Alan Such
225 Jean R. Gill
226 Mrs B. Bailey
227 Mary & Tom Berry
228 S. Johnson
229 Mr Ravenscroft
230 Mrs B. Walshaw
231 K. Andrews
232 G. Jones
233 Mrs Kinsey
234
235 - Mrs E. Whitney
236 Peter Tierney
237 Mrs T.J. Whitehead
238 Robert Palin
239 Joyce Such
240 Allan Breeze
241
242 - Chris Winward
243 High Street CP School
244 Brian O'Connor
245 Rosemary Ackerley
246 Eric J. Hulse
247 Mr & Mrs R.L. Antrobus
248 Leonard Weedall
249 Mary Curry
250 Mrs Done
251 Keith Edward Knight
252 E. Weedall
253 C.L. Dutton
254 E. Bratt
255 Keith Preston
256 Mr & Mrs W.D. Hewitt
257 Susan Rutter
258 Ann V. Long
259 Gillian Moore
260 Mrs C. Fowles
261 Mrs M. Murphy
262 Mr Kirk
263 Mrs Clewes
264 Mrs Mary Bogue
265 Matthew Clarke
266 T. Robinson
267 Irene Batin

268 Valerie & Barry
    Nurcombe
269 E.R. Parry
270 Janis Dean
271 G. Hatton
272
273 - Mrs Mellor
274 John Knight
275 Mrs S. Meredith
276 Mrs M. Perry
277 S. Littler
278 Mrs Dean
279 Mr Hazlehurst
280 Mrs Lycett
281 Phyllis Kolyn
282 Luke Green
383 John Hannon
284 Sam Hulse
285 Ronald Hamlett
286 Freda Brereton
287 Cal Withers
288 Allen Scanlan
289 James T. Williams
290 P. Greenhalgh
291 C. Bukojemski
292
293 - Mrs Dean
294- J. Carter
295
296 - Michael Austin
297 P. Scanlan
298 Mrs Wallis
299 G. Mellor
300 Mrs Forsey
301 J. Pritchard
302 Mrs Lightfoot
303 K. Higginson
304 Jack Parker
305 Peter Brandon
306 Keith J. Howbrigg
307 Andrew Meynell Adams
308 Mrs E. Reeves
309 Miss C. Hough
310 Mrs Egerton
311 A. Downes
312 Mrs P. Khadim
313 Bruce Crawford
314 Anthony Yearsley
315 Dorothy Phillips
316 Peter W. Mann
317 Mrs V. McCormack
318 Horace & Vera Wright
319 Christine E. Shepherd
320 Dr B.M. Sinclair
321 Keele University Library
322 Elizabeth Pardo
323 R.T. Coates
324 Steve Salisbury
325 Vince & Pamela Wilkinson
Remaining names unlisted.

END PAPERS – FRONT LEFT: Burdett's Map published in 1777;
RIGHT: Calvert's map of salt works and railways in 1870. BACK
LEFT: 1960s Winsford Town Map and RIGHT: and 1990s.

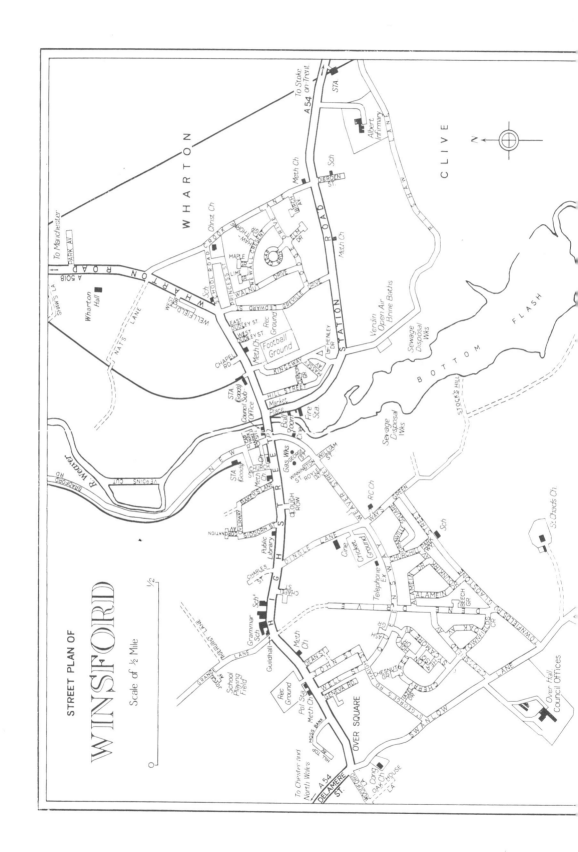

STREET PLAN OF

WINSFORD

Scale of ½ Mile